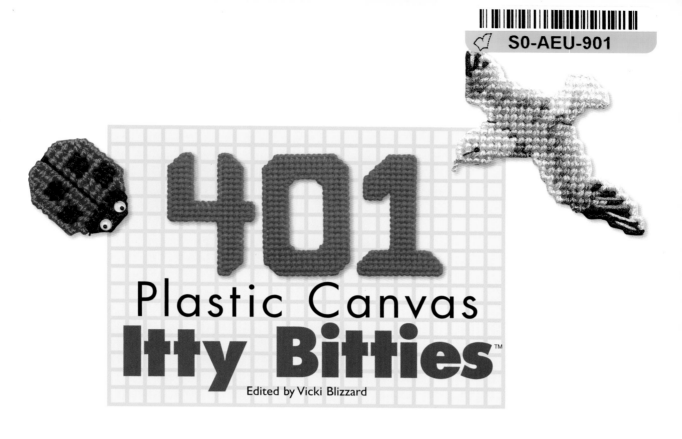

401
Plastic Canvas
Itty Bitties™

Edited by Vicki Blizzard

401 Plastic Canvas Itty Bitties

Copyright © 2005 House of White Birches, Berne, Indiana 46711

Editor: Vicki Blizzard
Art Director: Brad Snow
Publishing Services Manager: Brenda Gallmeyer

Associate Editor: Tanya Fox
Copy Supervisor: Michelle Beck
Copy Editors: Conor Allen, Nicki Lehman,
Mary Martin, Beverly Richardson
Technical Editor: June Sprunger

Graphic Arts Supervisor: Ronda Bechinski
Book Design: Karen Allen
Graphic Artists: Glenda Chamberlain, Edith Teegarden
Production Assistants: Cheryl Kempf, Marj Morgan

Photography: Tammy Christian, Carl Clark, Christena Green, Matt Owen
Photo Stylist: Tammy Nussbaum

Chief Executive Officer: John Robinson
Publishing Director: David McKee
Editorial Director: Vivian Rothe
Book Marketing Director: Craig Scott

Printed in China
First Printing: 2005
Library of Congress Number: 2004105953
Hardcover ISBN: 1-57367-175-4
Softcover ISBN: 1-57367-200-9

1 2 3 4 5 6 7 8 9

Welcome

Dear Stitching Friends,

I love plastic canvas stitching, and I know you do, too! If you're like me, you save every spare piece of plastic mesh and every extra yard of leftover yarn—just knowing that you'll find a pattern for it one of these days. That day is here!

This book has hundreds of itty-bitty projects—401 of them, in fact. None of them is larger than 25 holes square, and none of them uses more than a few yards of yarn. Each is quick to create with easy, familiar stitches, and you'll be able to create several of them in just one evening.

Choose your favorite and add a hanging cord to create a unique ornament. Or glue a magnet to the back of one to display on your filing cabinet at work. How about attaching one to a gift basket as a pretty embellishment? The largest of these can even be backed with cork or felt and used as coasters.

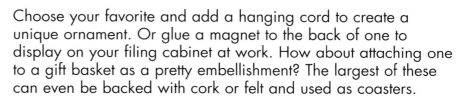

These versatile projects encompass every design style—traditional to whimsical to abstract, and everything in between. This book is conveniently divided into sections that will make it easy to find the type of motif you're looking for.

I hope you love these designs as much as I do and that you have fun choosing just the right ones to stitch!

Warm regards,

Vicki Blizzard

Contents

Critters

These animals have big person-alities in their little bodies.

page 8

Florals

Create a bouquet of tiny posies with these quick-to-stitch patterns!

page 28

Minis

Miscellaneous miniature projects include quilt blocks and abstract motifs.

page 36

Girls, Girls, Girls

Dainty projects for girls can be stitched in no time at all!

page 74

Holidays

Create a bevy of ornaments for all your holiday decorating.

page 92

General Instructions

page 6

Babies

Stitch one of these little projects as a last-minute baby shower gift add-on.

page 45

Boys' Toys

Boys of all ages will appreciate these manly-men designs.

page 57

By the Sea

Create these projects as reminders of summer vacation.

page 123

Munchies

These no-cal treats make great refrigerator magnets!

page 136

This & That

We didn't want to leave anything out, so we put these projects in their own category!

page 148

Special Thanks....172   Buyer's Guide.....173   Stitch Guide........174

General Instructions

1. All projects are made with 7-count, clear plastic canvas unless otherwise stated.

2. Check color keys and graphs for products, manufacturers and amounts before beginning a project. Color keys will list products and yardage. Graphs will show the amounts in the number of attachment points for each embellishment. Patterns (Pages 164–171) will give the medium used with each pattern.

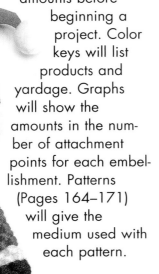

3. Stitch and Overcast all pieces following graphs and color keys, making sure to work all background stitching (including uncoded areas/backgrounds) and Overcasting before working the embroidery.

4. Unless otherwise designated, shapes, such as a diamond, triangle, square, heart, star, pentagon, hexagon and inverted triangle, represent Continental Stitches.

5. For "Cut Turkey Loop Stitches," cut all loops and separate yarn with a needle; brush and trim lightly.

Embellishments

1. Work all stitching before attaching embellishments. Use photos as guides for placement.

2. Attach beads, bells and buttons with beading or hand-sewing needle and matching thread. Use glue of choice for split beads and other attachments.

3. For pearl cotton or yarn antennae, stiffen by saturating fiber with thick white glue. Remove excess by pressing between fingers. Shape and allow to dry. Trim or knot as desired. To finish yarn end on shoelaces, fire hose, etc., dip ends in thick white glue, remove excess and allow to dry. As an alternative, wrap end with yarn or metallic cord.

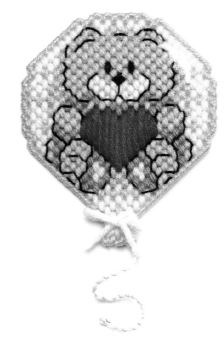

4. When craft/paddle wire is called for, use photo as a guide for lengths when not indicated and for shaping.

5. Paint wooden wheels, hubcaps, half beads for faces, etc. as desired following photos. (See instructions below for splitting wooden beads.)

6. Add embellishments not given in keys or graphs as desired, such as small amount short faux fur for tips of tails, etc.

Balloon Bear String

1. Fold wire in half. Place ½ yard/0.46m against one side of wire. Beginning at loop end, evenly twist remaining half of wire around yarn/wire. Trim yarn ends and curl raw end.

2. Curl string as desired. Attach loop end to back of balloon end where indicated.

Seagull Beak

1. Secure one end light old gold #3 pearl cotton on backside of stitching then thread through hole indicated to front, pulling firmly.

2. Twist pearl cotton in opposite directions until it begins to loop back on itself. Fold in half and thread needle end back through stitching behind placement point, allowing halves to twist around each other. Adjust bill length and secure thread.

Split Wooden Beads

1. Place a screwdriver over hole at top of bead. Tap top of screwdriver with a hammer to split bead.

Twisted Yarn

1. Cut approximately twice as much yarn as length desired. Tie ends together in a knot, forming a large circle.

2. Loop circle over index fingers of both hands. Twist fingers in opposite directions, twisting cord until it begins to loop back on itself. Place both loops on one index finger, folding yarn in half; allow halves to twist around each other.

Tassels

1. To create a 2-inch tassel, wrap several yards of yarn around a 4-inch piece of heavy cardboard. Slide loops off cardboard.

2. Cut a separate 12-inch piece of yarn and thread through center of loops; tie tightly.

3. Cut another 12-inch piece of yarn and tie around top of tassel, approximately ½ inch from fold at top of tassel.

4. Trim ends of tassel to desired length.

Polymer Clay Noses

1. To create pointy noses for snowmen and other characters, pinch off a small piece of orange polymer clay and roll between fingers until warm.

2. Roll clay into a ball. Pinch one end of ball until pointed (the ball is now a teardrop shape).

3. Bake shape according to manufacturer's instructions.

Note: *Vary the look of noses by making some very long and some short. Try making tiny round balls for some noses.*

Finishing

1. Finish projects by adding felt backing, hangers, garlands or magnet as desired.

Critters

These tiny animals are fun to stitch! Use them as plant pokes to add a bit of whimsical wildlife to your home.

Puffy Kitty

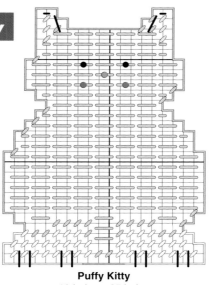

Puffy Kitty
19 holes x 25 holes
Cut 1

Cottontail

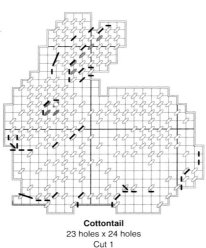

Cottontail
23 holes x 24 holes
Cut 1

Duck

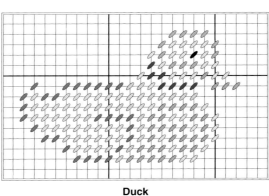

Duck
25 holes x 16 holes
Cut 1

Gray Squirrel

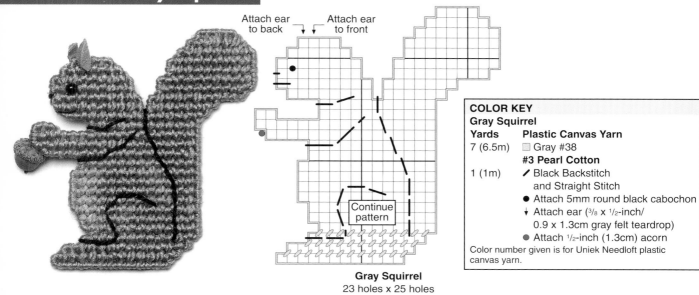

Attach ear to back
Attach ear to front

Continue pattern

Gray Squirrel
23 holes x 25 holes
Cut 1

COLOR KEY
Gray Squirrel

Yards	Plastic Canvas Yarn
7 (6.5m)	☐ Gray #38

#3 Pearl Cotton

1 (1m)	╱ Black Backstitch and Straight Stitch
	● Attach 5mm round black cabochon
	↓ Attach ear (³⁄₈ x ¹⁄₂-inch/ 0.9 x 1.3cm gray felt teardrop)
	● Attach ¹⁄₂-inch (1.3cm) acorn

Color number given is for Uniek Needloft plastic canvas yarn.

Ducky

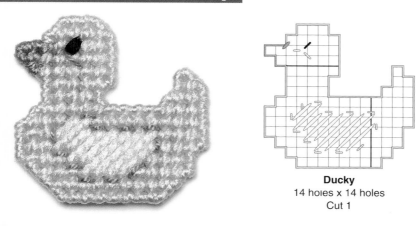

Ducky
14 holes x 14 holes
Cut 1

COLOR KEY
Ducky

Yards	Plastic Canvas Yarn
1 (1m)	☐ Pumpkin #12
1 (1m)	☐ Lemon #20
3 (2.8m)	Uncoded areas are yellow #57 Continental Stitches
	╱ Yellow #57 Overcasting

#5 Pearl Cotton

| 1 (1m) | ╱ Pumpkin Backstitch and Running Stitch |

6-Strand Embroidery Floss

| 1 (1m) | ╱ Black Straight Stitch (3 times) |

Color numbers given are for Uniek Needloft plastic canvas yarn.

Big Bee

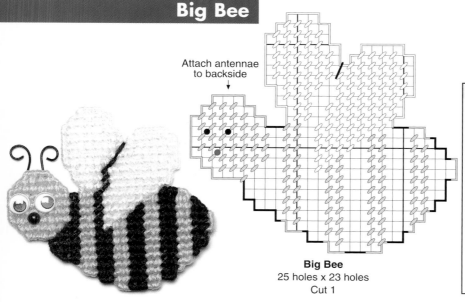

Attach antennae to backside

Big Bee
25 holes x 23 holes
Cut 1

COLOR KEY
Big Bee

Yards	Plastic Canvas Yarn
3 (2.8m)	■ Black #00
4 (3.7m)	☐ White #41
4 (3.7m)	☐ Yellow #57
	Uncoded areas are black #00 Continental Stitches Black #00 Backstitch and Overcasting
	● Attach 10mm round movable eye
	● Attach 5mm round black cabochon
	↓ Attach antennae (5 inches/12.7cm 20-gauge black craft wire)

Color numbers given are for Uniek Needloft plastic canvas yarn.

Giant Ladybug

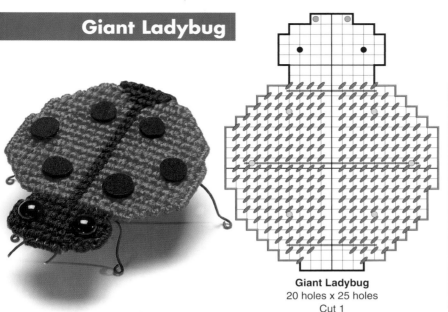

Giant Ladybug
20 holes x 25 holes
Cut 1

COLOR KEY
Giant Ladybug

Yards	Plastic Canvas Yarn
2 (1.9m)	■ Red #01
7 (6.5m)	Uncoded areas are black #00 Continental Stitches
	╱ Black #00 Overcasting
	● Attach 10mm round black cabochons
	○ Attach spots (10mm black craft foam circles)
	● Attach 1-inch/2.5cm antenna (20-gauge/.88mm bare paddle wire)
	– Attach legs to backside (20-gauge/ .88m bare paddle wire)

Color numbers given are for Uniek Needloft plastic canvas yarn.

White-Winged Bee

Illustrations on page 164

White-Winged Bee
10 holes x 12 holes
Cut 1

COLOR KEY
White-Winged Bee

Yards	Plastic Canvas Yarn
2 (1.9m)	☐ Yellow #57
1 (1m)	Uncoded areas are black #00 Continental Stitches
	╱ Black #00 Overcasting
	⊙ Attach 7mm white craft foam circle under 5mm round black cabochon
	● Attach black seed bead
	○ Attach small wing in front of large wing (see patterns)
	● Thread antennae (22-gauge/.73mm black craft wire) from bottom to top
	– Attach legs to backside (22-gauge/ .73mm black craft wire)

Color numbers given are for Uniek Needloft plastic canvas yarn.

Garden Worm

Garden Worm
25 holes x 25 holes
Cut 1

COLOR KEY
Garden Worm

Yards	Plastic Canvas Yarn
7 (6.5m)	■ Fern #23
1 (1m)	☐ Watermelon #55
	6-Strand Embroidery Floss
1 (1m)	╱ Black Backstitch
	● Attach 4mm hot pink bead
	⊙ Attach 7mm white craft foam circle under 5mm round black cabochon
	↓ Attach antenna (18-gauge/ 1.21mm green craft wire)

Color numbers given are for Uniek Needloft plastic canvas yarn.

Snow-White Dove

Illustration on page 164

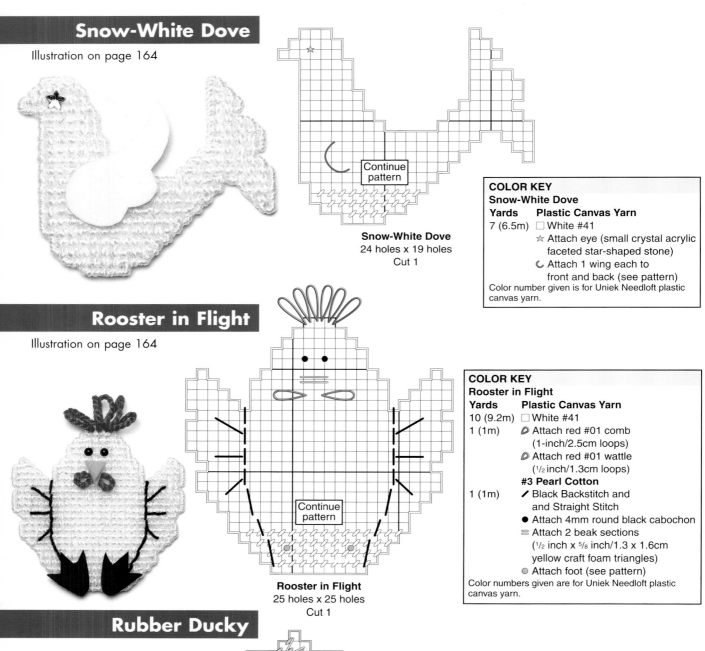

Snow-White Dove
24 holes x 19 holes
Cut 1

COLOR KEY
Snow-White Dove

Yards	Plastic Canvas Yarn
7 (6.5m)	☐ White #41

☆ Attach eye (small crystal acrylic
faceted star-shaped stone)

☾ Attach 1 wing each to
front and back (see pattern)

Color number given is for Uniek Needloft plastic
canvas yarn.

Rooster in Flight

Illustration on page 164

Rooster in Flight
25 holes x 25 holes
Cut 1

COLOR KEY
Rooster in Flight

Yards	Plastic Canvas Yarn
10 (9.2m)	☐ White #41
1 (1m)	◑ Attach red #01 comb (1-inch/2.5cm loops)
	◑ Attach red #01 wattle (½ inch/1.3cm loops)

#3 Pearl Cotton

1 (1m)	╱ Black Backstitch and and Straight Stitch
	● Attach 4mm round black cabochon
	═ Attach 2 beak sections (½ inch x ⅝ inch/1.3 x 1.6cm yellow craft foam triangles)
	● Attach foot (see pattern)

Color numbers given are for Uniek Needloft plastic
canvas yarn.

Rubber Ducky

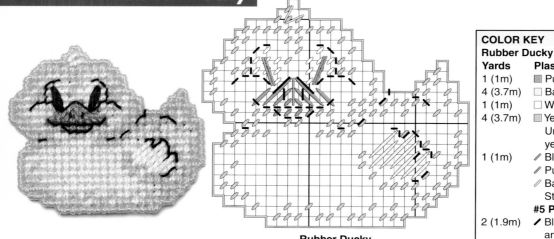

Rubber Ducky
25 holes x 22 holes
Cut 1

COLOR KEY
Rubber Ducky

Yards	Plastic Canvas Yarn
1 (1m)	▨ Pumpkin #12
4 (3.7m)	☐ Baby yellow #21
1 (1m)	☐ White #41
4 (3.7m)	▨ Yellow #57
	Uncoded areas are baby yellow #21 Continental Stitches
1 (1m)	╱ Black #00 Straight Stitch
	╱ Pumpkin #12 Straight Stitch
	╱ Baby yellow #21 Straight Stitch

#5 Pearl Cotton

2 (1.9m)	╱ Black Backstitch and Straight Stitch

Color numbers given are for Uniek Needloft
plastic canvas yarn.

Fantasy Bird

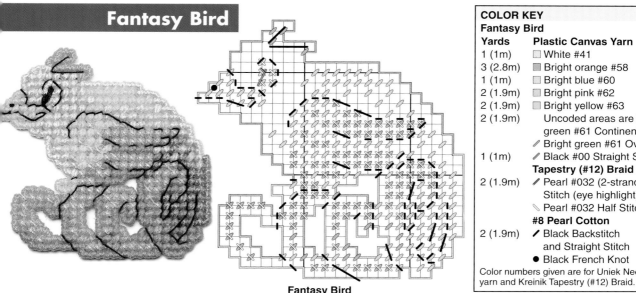

Fantasy Bird
25 holes x 25 holes
Cut 1

COLOR KEY
Fantasy Bird

Yards	Plastic Canvas Yarn
1 (1m)	□ White #41
3 (2.8m)	■ Bright orange #58
1 (1m)	□ Bright blue #60
2 (1.9m)	□ Bright pink #62
2 (1.9m)	□ Bright yellow #63
2 (1.9m)	Uncoded areas are bright green #61 Continental Stitches
	∕ Bright green #61 Overcasting
1 (1m)	∕ Black #00 Straight Stitch
	Tapestry (#12) Braid
2 (1.9m)	∕ Pearl #032 (2-strand) Straight Stitch (eye highlight)
	∖ Pearl #032 Half Stitch
	#8 Pearl Cotton
2 (1.9m)	∕ Black Backstitch and Straight Stitch
	● Black French Knot

Color numbers given are for Uniek Needloft plastic yarn and Kreinik Tapestry (#12) Braid.

Little Ladybug

Little Ladybug
9 holes x 11 holes
Cut 1

COLOR KEY
Little Ladybug

Yards	Plastic Canvas Yarn
1 (1m)	■ Black #00
2 (1.9m)	■ Christmas red #02
	6-Strand Embroidery Floss
	∕ Black Backstitch
	● Attach 5mm round movable eye
	○ Attach antennae from back to front (1½-inch/3.8mm-long florist wire colored with black marker)

Color numbers given are for Uniek Needloft plastic canvas yarn.

Mr. Gobbler

Illustrations on page 164

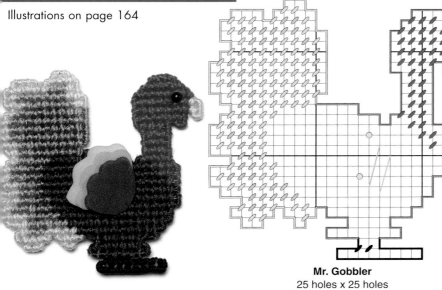

Mr. Gobbler
25 holes x 25 holes
Cut 1

COLOR KEY
Mr. Gobbler

Yards	Plastic Canvas Yarn
1 (1m)	■ Black #00
1 (1m)	■ Christmas red #02
1 (1m)	□ Rust #09
1 (1m)	□ Camel #43
2 (1.9m)	□ Yellow #57
3 (2.8m)	Uncoded areas are cinnamon #14 Continental Stitches
	∕ Cinnamon #14 Overcasting
	● Attach 5mm round black cabochon
	○ Attach yellow wing (see pattern)
	∕ Attach orange wing (see pattern)
	∕ Attach brown wing (see pattern)

Color numbers given are for Uniek Needloft plastic canvas yarn.

Smiling Frog

Smiling Frog
25 holes x 25 holes
Cut 1

Pocket-Pal Frog

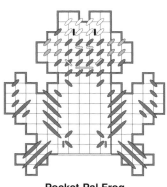

Pocket-Pal Frog
15 holes x 16 holes
Cut 1

Tiny Tiger

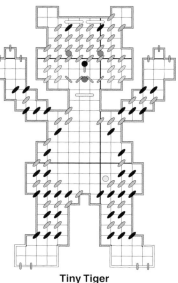

Tiny Tiger
17 holes x 25 holes
Cut 1

Long-Tailed Rooster

Illustrations on page 165

Attach comb to backside

Attach beak

Continue pattern

Long-Tailed Rooster
18 holes x 25 holes
Cut 1

Sitting Bunny

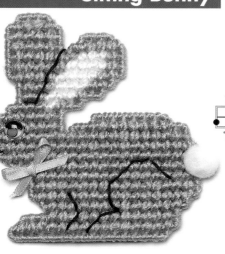

Sitting Bunny
20 holes x 22 holes
Cut 1

Spring Chicken

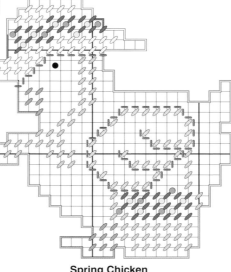

Spring Chicken
23 holes x 25 holes
Cut 1

Plaid Butterfly

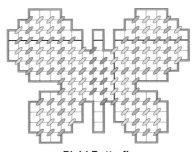

Plaid Butterfly
17 holes x 13 holes
Cut 1

Fantasy Bug

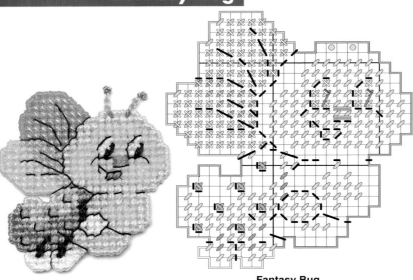

Fantasy Bug
23 holes x 25 holes
Cut 1

Peeking Cat

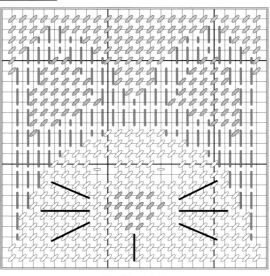

Peeking Cat
25 holes x 25 holes
Cut 1

Blue-Eyed Bunny

Blue-Eyed Bunny
21 holes x 25 holes
Cut 1

Hummingbird

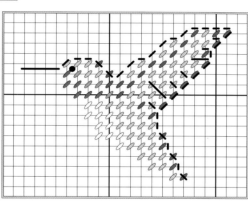

Hummingbird
23 holes x 18 holes
Cut 1

Wide-Eyed Duck

Illustration on page 165

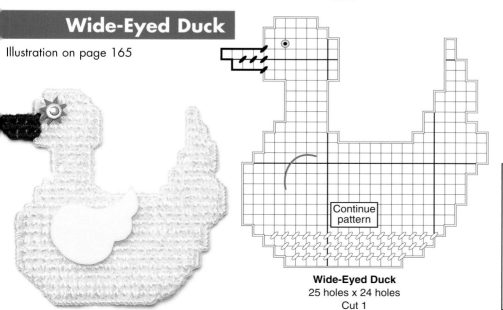

Continue pattern

Wide-Eyed Duck
25 holes x 24 holes
Cut 1

Spot

Illustration on page 165

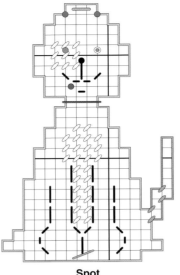

Spot
16 holes x 25 holes
Cut 1

COLOR KEY
Spot

Yards	Plastic Canvas Yarn
1 (1m)	■ Black #00
1 (1m)	□ White #41
4 (3.7m)	Uncoded areas are camel #43 Continental Stitches
	⁄ Camel #43 Overcasting
	⬭ Camel #43 (³/₈-inch/1cm-long) Cut Turkey Loop Stitch

#3 Pearl Cotton

1 (1m)	⁄ Black Backstitch and Straight Stitch
	● Attach 6mm round black cabochon
	● Attach 6mm brown animal eye
	◉ Attach 7mm white felt circle under 6mm brown animal eye
	● Attach tongue (small piece red faux suede)
	● Attach ear
	⁄ Attach miniature (or button) bone
	⁄ Attach ³/₁₆-inch-wide (0.5cm) strip brown faux suede

Color numbers given are for Uniek Needloft plastic canvas yarn.

Yellow Duck

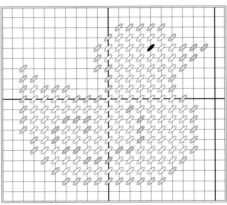

Yellow Duck
21 holes x 19 holes
Cut 1

COLOR KEY
Yellow Duck

Yards	Worsted Weight Yarn
2 (1.9m)	▨ Orange #245
1 (1m)	■ Black #312
4 (3.7m)	□ Pale yellow #322
1 (1.9m)	▨ Bright yellow #324
1 (1m)	▨ Petal pink #373
3 (2.8m)	Uncoded background is pale green #363 Continental Stitches
	⁄ Pale green #363 Overcasting

Color numbers given are for Coats & Clark Red Heart Classic worsted weight yarn Art. E267 and Super Saver worsted weight yarn Art. E300.

Black Cat

Glue tip of tail behind head

Black Cat
18 holes x 25 holes
Cut 1

COLOR KEY
Black Cat

Yards	Plastic Canvas Yarn
1 (1m)	□ Pink #07
2 (1.9m)	□ White #41
1 (1m)	▨ Gray #38
5 (4.6m)	Uncoded areas are black #00 Continental Stitches
	⁄ Black #00 Overcasting

#3 Pearl Cotton

1 (1m)	⁄ Black Backstitch
	◉ Attach 9mm blue cat eye
	● Attach 6mm round black cabochon
	○ Attach tongue (tiny piece pink craft foam)
	○ Attach ¹/₄-inch/6mm gold jingle bell
	▨ Brush yarn in this area with pink blush

Color numbers given are for Uniek Needloft plastic canvas yarn.

Silly Turtle

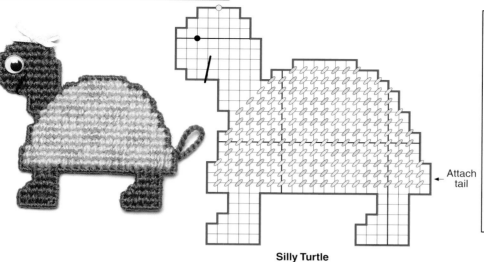

Silly Turtle
24 holes x 23 holes
Cut 1

Attach tail

COLOR KEY
Silly Turtle

Yards	Plastic Canvas Yarn
3 (2.8m)	☐ Pink #07
3 (2.8m)	☐ Bright green #61
3 (2.8m)	Uncoded areas are holly #27 Continental Stitches
	╱ Holly #27 Overcasting

#5 Pearl Cotton
╱ Black Straight Stitch
← Attach tail (holly #27 1-inch/2.5cm loop)
○ Attach tiny pink ribbon bow
● Attach 10 mm round movable eye

Color numbers given are for Uniek Needloft plastic canvas yarn.

Decorated Ducky

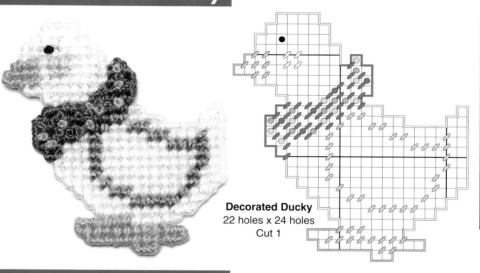

Decorated Ducky
22 holes x 24 holes
Cut 1

COLOR KEY
Decorated Ducky

Yards	Plastic Canvas Yarn
1 (1m)	☐ Pink #07
1 (1m)	☐ Tangerine #11
1 (1m)	■ Christmas green #28
1 (1m)	☐ Gray #38
3 (2.8m)	Uncoded areas are white #41 Continental Stitches
	╱ White #41 Overcasting
1 (1m)	● Black #00 French Knot
1 (1m)	● Royal #32 French Knot
1 (1m)	● Watermelon #55 French Knot
1 (1m)	○ Yellow #57 French Knot

Color numbers given are for Uniek Needloft plastic canvas yarn.

Bouncing Bunny

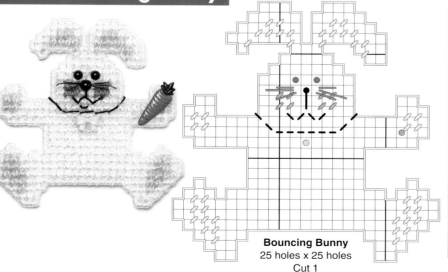

Bouncing Bunny
25 holes x 25 holes
Cut 1

COLOR KEY
Bouncing Bunny

Yards	Plastic Canvas Yarn
2 (1.9m)	☐ Pink #07
1 (1m)	☐ Watermelon #55
7 (6.5m)	Uncoded areas are white #41 Continental Stitches
	╱ White #41 Overcasting

6-Strand Embroidery Floss

1 (1m)	╱ Black (3-ply) Backstitch and Straight Stitch
	╱ Black (1-ply) Straight Stitch
	● Attach 5mm round black cabochon
	● Attach 6mm round black cabochon
	○ Attach miniature (or button) bow tie
	● Attach miniature (or button) carrot

Color numbers given are for Uniek Needloft plastic canvas yarn.

Raccoon

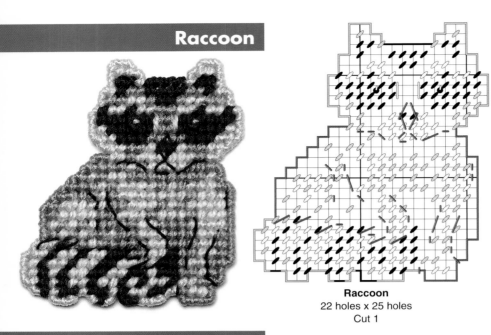

COLOR KEY
Raccoon

Yards	Plastic Canvas Yarn
2 (1.9m)	■ Black #00
3 (2.8m)	▨ Silver #37
2 (1.9m)	☐ Eggshell #39
3 (2.8m)	Uncoded areas are gray #38 Continental Stitches
	╱ Gray #38 Overcasting
	╱ Silver #37 (1-ply) Straight Stitch
	╱ Eggshell #39 (4-ply) Straight Stitch
	● Black #00 (4-ply) French Knot
2 (1.9m)	**#5 Pearl Cotton**
	╱ Black Backstitch and Straight Stitch

Color numbers given are for Uniek Needloft plastic canvas yarn.

Raccoon
22 holes x 25 holes
Cut 1

Lovebird

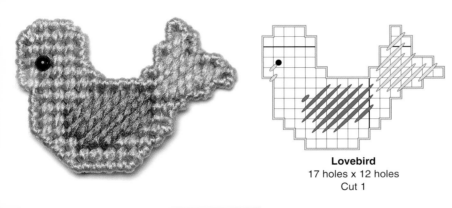

COLOR KEY
Lovebird

Yards	Plastic Canvas Yarn
1 (1m)	■ Turquoise #54
1 (1m)	☐ Yellow #57
2 (1.9m)	☐ Bright blue #60
	Uncoded areas are bright blue #60 Continental Stitches
	● Attach 5mm round black cabochon

Color numbers given are for Uniek Needloft plastic canvas yarn.

Lovebird
17 holes x 12 holes
Cut 1

Wise Old Owl

Illustration on page 165

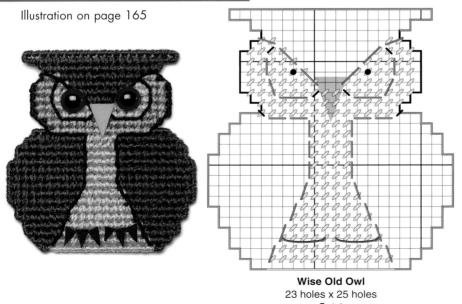

COLOR KEY
Wise Old Owl

Yards	Plastic Canvas Yarn
1 (1m)	☐ Sandstone #16
2 (1.9m)	☐ Beige #40
2 (1.9m)	☐ Yellow #57
6 (5.5m)	Uncoded areas are cinnamon #14 Continental Stitches
1 (1m)	╱ Black #00 Overcasting
	╱ Cinnamon #14 Overcasting
	#3 Pearl Cotton
1 (1m)	╱ Black Backstitch
	● Attach 12mm brown animal eyes
	▼ Attach beak (7/16 x 5/8 inches/1.1 x 1.6cm orange craft foam triangle)
	⌣ Attach foot (see pattern)

Color numbers given are for Uniek Needloft plastic canvas yarn.

Wise Old Owl
23 holes x 25 holes
Cut 1

Hungry Bunny

Illustrations on page 165

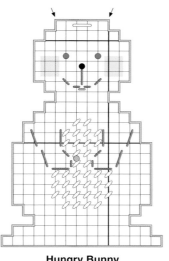

Hungry Bunny
15 holes x 22 holes
Cut 1

Leopold

Illustration on page 166

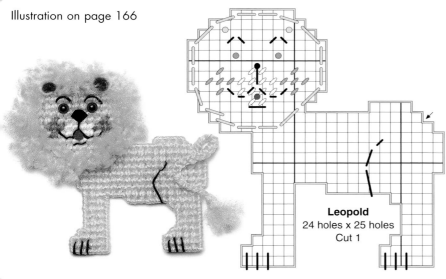

Leopold
24 holes x 25 holes
Cut 1

Chipper

Chipper
21 holes x 25 holes
Cut 1

Continue pattern

Pretty Pony

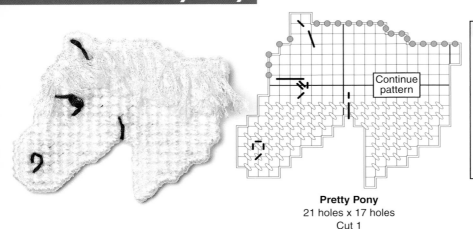

Pretty Pony
21 holes x 17 holes
Cut 1

COLOR KEY

Pretty Pony

Yards	Plastic Canvas Yarn
4 (3.7m)	☐ White #41
	Iridescent Craft Cord
2 (1.9m)	● Attach 1-inch/2.5cm-long mane (white #55033 Lark's Head Knot)
	6-Strand Embroidery Floss
1 (1m)	✐ Black Backstitch and Straight Stitch

Color numbers given are for Uniek Needloft plastic canvas yarn and iridescent craft cord.

Portly Pig

Illustrations on page 166

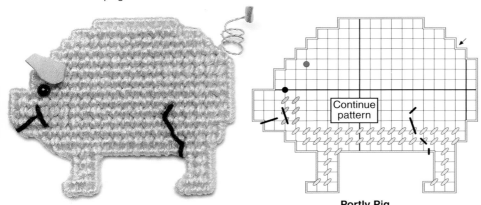

Portly Pig
21 holes x 17 holes
Cut 1

COLOR KEY

Portly Pig

Yards	Plastic Canvas Yarn
1 (1m)	☐ Pink #07
7 (6.5m)	☐ Pale peach #56
	#3 Pearl Cotton
1 (1m)	✐ Black Backstitch and Straight Stitch
	● Attach 5mm round black cabochon
	● Attach ear (see pattern)
	✐ Attach tail with tip (26-gauge/ 46mm coiled pink craft wire) (see pattern)

Color numbers given are for Uniek Needloft plastic canvas yarn.

Mansfield the Mouse

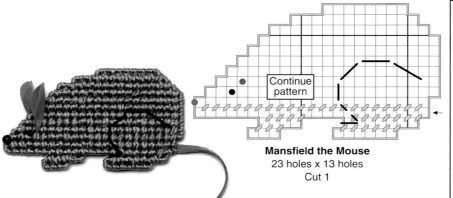

Mansfield the Mouse
23 holes x 13 holes
Cut 1

COLOR KEY

Mansfield the Mouse

Yards	Plastic Canvas Yarn
5 (4.6m)	☐ Gray #38
	6-Strand Embroidery Floss
1 (1m)	✐ Black Backstitch
	● Black French Knot
	● Attach 5mm round black cabochon
	● Attach 1 ear each to front and back (⅝ x 1 inch/1.6 x 2.5cm gray faux suede or felt teardrop)
	← Attach tail to back (narrow 4¼-inch/10.8cm-long gray faux suede or felt triangle)

Color number given is for Uniek Needloft plastic canvas yarn.

Bunny & Blossoms

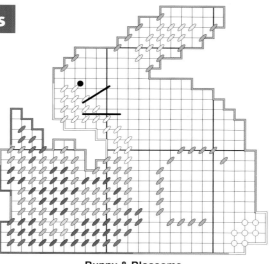

Bunny & Blossoms
25 holes x 24 holes
Cut 1

COLOR KEY
Bunny & Blossoms

Yards	Plastic Canvas Yarn
1 (1m)	☐ Pink #07
1 (1m)	☐ Maple #13
1 (1m)	☐ Christmas green #28
1 (1m)	☐ White #41
1 (1m)	☐ Bittersweet #52
1 (1m)	☐ Yellow #57
1 (1m)	☐ Bright orange #58
3 (2.8m)	Uncoded area is sandstone #16 Continental Stitches
1 (1m)	╱ Black #00 Straight Stitch
	● Black #00 French Knot
	○ White #41 French Knot

Color numbers given are for Uniek Needloft plastic canvas yarn.

Bitty Bunny

Bitty Bunny
14 holes x 14 holes
Cut 1

COLOR KEY
Bitty Bunny

Yards	Plastic Canvas Yarn
1 (1m)	☐ Pink #07
2 (1.9m)	☐ Gray #38
1 (1m)	╱ Watermelon #55 Straight Stitch
	6-Strand Embroidery Floss
1 (1m)	╱ Black Backstitch
	╱ Black Straight Stitch (2 times)

Color numbers given are for Uniek Needloft plastic canvas yarn.

Puffy Bunny

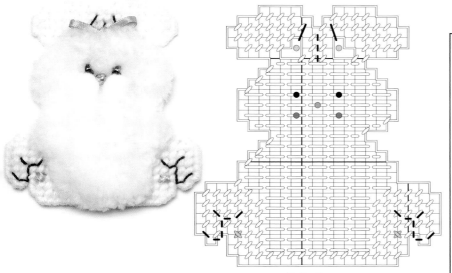

Puffy Bunny
23 holes x 25 holes
Cut 1

COLOR KEY
Puffy Bunny

Yards	Worsted Weight Yarn
12 (11m)	☐ White #1
	⌣ White #1 (⅝-inch/1.6cm-long) Cut Turkey Loop Stitch
	⅛-Inch/0.3cm-Wide Satin Ribbon
1 (1m)	☐ Rose
	◎ Thread 5-inch/12.7cm length rose from back to front and tie in bow
	#5 Pearl Cotton
1 (1m)	╱ Black Backstitch and Straight Stitch
	● Attach ½-inch/10mm white pompom
	● Attach new penny #05555 glass pebble bead
	● Attach black frost #05081 glass pebble bead

Color numbers given are for Coats & Clark Red Heart Classic worsted weight yarn Art. E267 and Mill Hill Products glass pebble beads from Gay Bowles Sales Inc.

Plump Penguin

Plump Penguin
24 holes x 25 holes
Cut 1

Perky Penguin

Perky Penguin
19 holes x 25 holes
Cut 1

Mr. Penguin

Mr. Penguin
20 holes x 24 holes
Cut 1

Chickadee

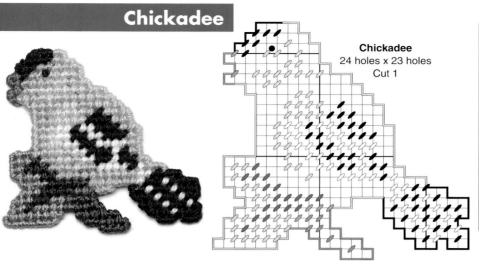

Chickadee
24 holes x 23 holes
Cut 1

COLOR KEY
Chickadee

Yards	Plastic Canvas Yarn
2 (1.9m)	■ Black #00
1 (1m)	■ Cinnamon #14
1 (1m)	■ Fern #23
1 (1m)	■ Forest #29
1 (1m)	□ White #41
1 (1m)	■ Bittersweet #52
1 (1m)	□ Yellow #57

Uncoded areas are tangerine #11 Continental Stitches
/ Tangerine #11 Overcasting
● Black #00 French Knot

Color numbers given are for Uniek Needloft plastic canvas yarn.

Bluebird

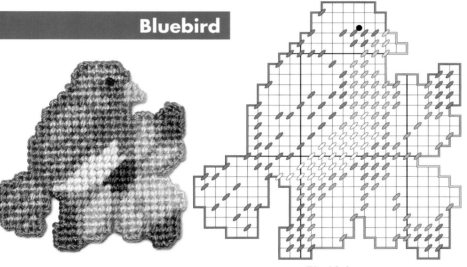

Bluebird
25 holes x 25 holes
Cut 1

COLOR KEY
Bluebird

Yards	Plastic Canvas Yarn
1 (1m)	□ Tangerine #11
1 (1m)	■ Pumpkin #12
1 (1m)	■ Cinnamon #14
1 (1m)	■ Christmas green #28
2 (1.9m)	■ Royal #32
1 (1m)	□ Eggshell #39
1 (1m)	■ Watermelon #55
2 (1.9m)	Uncoded areas on bird are sail blue #35 Continental Stitches
2 (1.9m)	Uncoded areas on flower are yellow #57 Continental Stitches
	/ Yellow #57 Overcasting
1 (1m)	● Black #00 French Knot

Color numbers given are for Uniek Needloft plastic canvas yarn.

Hummingbird & Flower

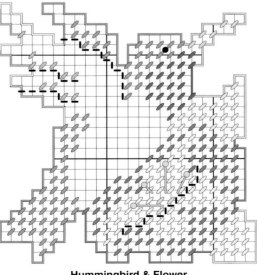

Hummingbird & Flower
24 holes x 25 holes
Cut 1

COLOR KEY
Hummingbird & Flower

Yards	Plastic Canvas Yarn
1 (1m)	■ Christmas red #02
2 (1.9m)	■ Fern #23
2 (1.9m)	■ Royal #32
1 (1m)	□ Sail blue #35
1 (1m)	■ Camel #43
1 (1m)	■ Mermaid #53
1 (1m)	□ Yellow #57
2 (1.9m)	Uncoded areas are eggshell #39 Continental Stitches
	/ Eggshell #39 Overcasting
1 (1m)	/ Black #00 Backstitch
	/ Yellow #57 Straight Stitch
	● Black #00 French Knot
	○ Yellow #57 French Knot

Color numbers given are for Uniek Needloft plastic canvas yarn.

Vintage Butterfly

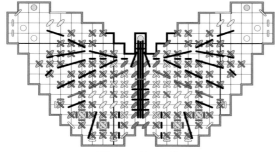

Vintage Butterfly
25 holes x 14 holes
Cut 1

Black Spider

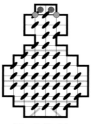

Black Spider
8 holes x 11 holes
Cut 1

Yellow Butterfly

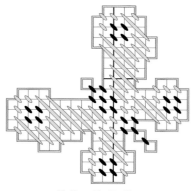

Yellow Butterfly
17 holes x 17 holes
Cut 1

Playful Bear

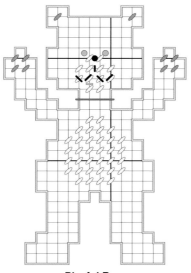

Playful Bear
17 holes x 25 holes
Cut 1

COLOR KEY
Playful Bear

Yards	Plastic Canvas Yarn
1 (1m)	■ Brown #15
2 (1.9m)	□ Eggshell #39
4 (3.7m)	Uncoded areas are camel #43 Continental Stitches
	⁄ Camel #43 Overcasting
	⁄ Watermelon #55 1/16-inch-long (0.2cm) loop
	6-Strand Embroidery Floss
1 (1m)	⁄ Black (3-ply) Backstitch
	● Attach 6mm round black cabochon
	◉ Attach 6mm brown animal eye
	⁄ Attach 3/16-inch-wide (0.5m) strip red faux suede

Color numbers given are for Uniek Needloft plastic canvas yarn.

Ornery Kitty

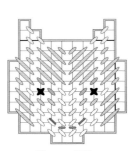

Ornery Kitty
11 holes x 12 holes
Cut 1

COLOR KEY
Ornery Kitty

Yards	Worsted Weight Yarn
2 (1.9m)	□ Gray
1 (1m)	□ Pink
1 (1m)	■ Black (2 plies)
1 (1m)	▨ Blue
1 (1m)	□ White
	⁄ Black (1-ply) Backstitch

Puffy Puppy

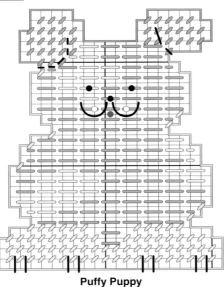

Puffy Puppy
21 holes x 25 holes
Cut 1

COLOR KEY
Puffy Puppy

Yards	Worsted Weight Yarn
10 (9.2m)	□ Tan #334
4 (3.7m)	■ Warm brown #336
	◠ Tan #334 (5/8-inch/1.6cm-long) Cut Turkey Loop Stitch
	◠ Warm brown #336 (5/8-inch/ 1.6cm-long) Cut Turkey Loop Stitch
	#5 Pearl Cotton
1 (1m)	⁄ Black Backstitch and Straight Stitch
	○ Attach 1/2-inch/10mm white pompom
	● Attach black frost #05081 glass pebble bead
	● Attach tongue (tiny scrap 1/8-inch/ 0.3cm-wide burgundy satin ribbon)

Color numbers given are for Coats & Clark Red Heart Classic worsted weight yarn Art. E267 and Mill Hill Products glass pebble beads from Gay Bowles Sales Inc.

■ **Critters** ■

Florals

Create everlasting blossoms with one of these easy-to-stitch flower motifs! Some of them are large enough to be used as elegant coasters!

Dandelion

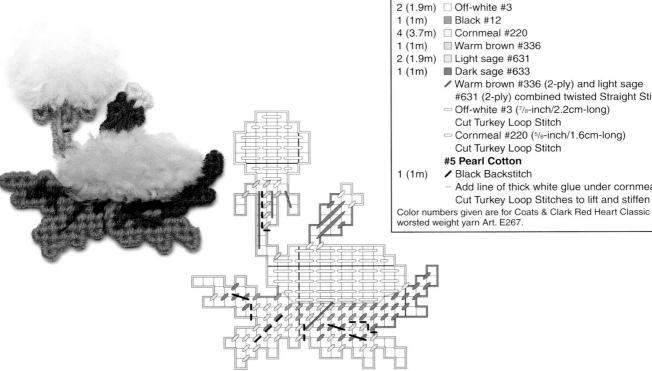

COLOR KEY
Dandelion

Yards	Worsted Weight Yarn
2 (1.9m)	☐ Off-white #3
1 (1m)	■ Black #12
4 (3.7m)	☐ Cornmeal #220
1 (1m)	☐ Warm brown #336
2 (1.9m)	☐ Light sage #631
1 (1m)	■ Dark sage #633
	⟋ Warm brown #336 (2-ply) and light sage #631 (2-ply) combined twisted Straight Stitch
	⌢ Off-white #3 (⅞-inch/2.2cm-long) Cut Turkey Loop Stitch
	⌢ Cornmeal #220 (⅝-inch/1.6cm-long) Cut Turkey Loop Stitch

#5 Pearl Cotton

1 (1m)	⟋ Black Backstitch
	– Add line of thick white glue under cornmeal Cut Turkey Loop Stitches to lift and stiffen

Color numbers given are for Coats & Clark Red Heart Classic worsted weight yarn Art. E267.

Dandelion
23 holes x 25 holes
Cut 1

Bicolored Floral

Bicolored Floral
25 holes x 25 holes
Cut 1

Continue pattern

COLOR KEY
Bicolored Floral

Yards	Worsted Weight Yarn
1 (1m)	■ Black #12
6 (5.5m)	☐ Lavender #584
1 (1m)	■ Paddy green #686
6 (5.5m)	☐ Lime #2652
3 (2.8m)	⌀ Pink #2734 Lazy Daisy Stitch

Color numbers given are for Coats & Clark Red Heart Classic worsted weight yarn Art. E267 and Kids worsted weight yarn Art. E711.

Cabbage Rose

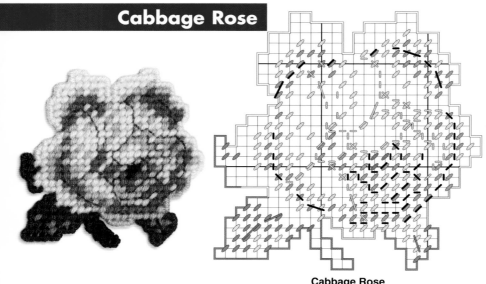

Cabbage Rose
25 holes x 25 holes
Cut 1

Daffodil

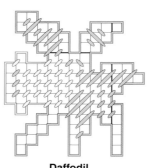

Daffodil
13 holes x 14 holes
Cut 1

Pansy Nosegay

Pansy Nosegay
25 holes x 25 holes
Cut 1

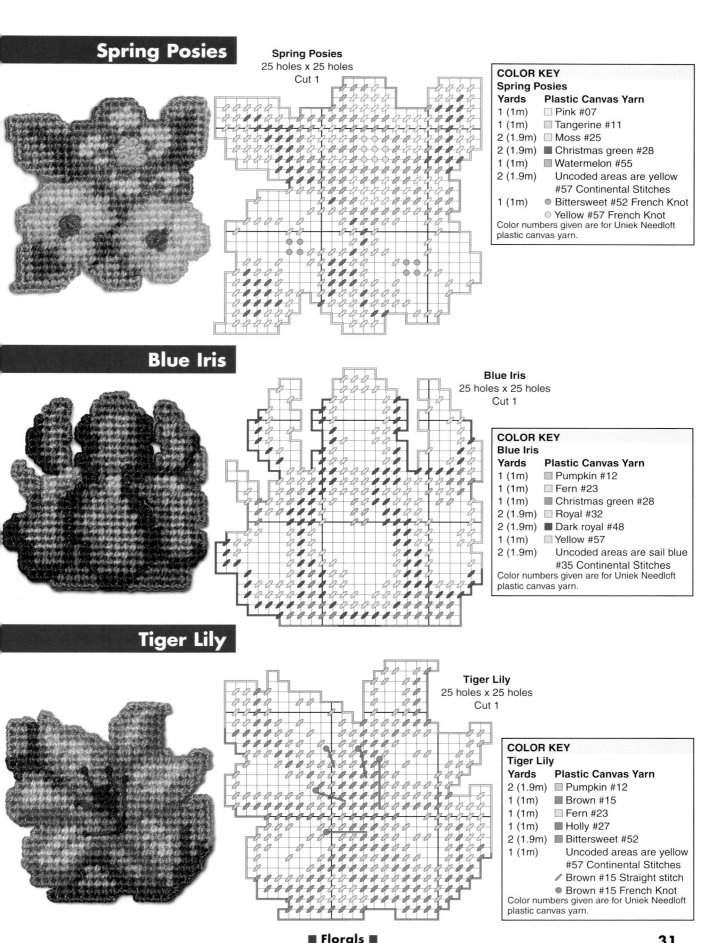

Spring Posies

Spring Posies
25 holes x 25 holes
Cut 1

COLOR KEY
Spring Posies

Yards	Plastic Canvas Yarn
1 (1m)	☐ Pink #07
1 (1m)	☐ Tangerine #11
2 (1.9m)	☐ Moss #25
2 (1.9m)	■ Christmas green #28
1 (1m)	☐ Watermelon #55
2 (1.9m)	Uncoded areas are yellow #57 Continental Stitches
1 (1m)	● Bittersweet #52 French Knot
	○ Yellow #57 French Knot

Color numbers given are for Uniek Needloft plastic canvas yarn.

Blue Iris

Blue Iris
25 holes x 25 holes
Cut 1

COLOR KEY
Blue Iris

Yards	Plastic Canvas Yarn
1 (1m)	☐ Pumpkin #12
1 (1m)	☐ Fern #23
1 (1m)	■ Christmas green #28
2 (1.9m)	☐ Royal #32
2 (1.9m)	■ Dark royal #48
1 (1m)	☐ Yellow #57
2 (1.9m)	Uncoded areas are sail blue #35 Continental Stitches

Color numbers given are for Uniek Needloft plastic canvas yarn.

Tiger Lily

Tiger Lily
25 holes x 25 holes
Cut 1

COLOR KEY
Tiger Lily

Yards	Plastic Canvas Yarn
2 (1.9m)	☐ Pumpkin #12
1 (1m)	■ Brown #15
1 (1m)	☐ Fern #23
1 (1m)	■ Holly #27
2 (1.9m)	■ Bittersweet #52
1 (1m)	Uncoded areas are yellow #57 Continental Stitches
	╱ Brown #15 Straight stitch
	● Brown #15 French Knot

Color numbers given are for Uniek Needloft plastic canvas yarn.

Purple Pansy

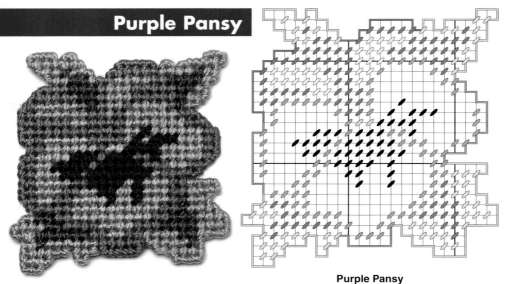

Purple Pansy
24 holes x 25 holes
Cut 1

Tulip Circle

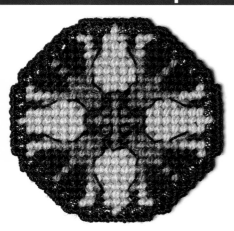

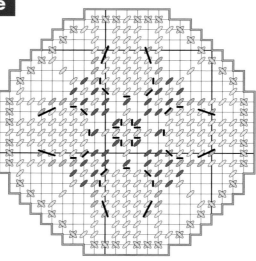

Tulip Circle
24 holes x 24 holes
Cut 1

Framed Rose

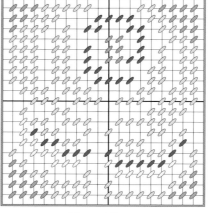

Framed Rose
19 holes x 20 holes
Cut 1

Iris

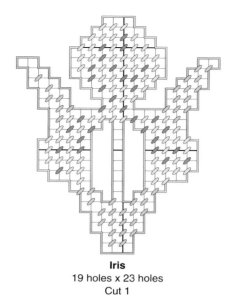

Iris
19 holes x 23 holes
Cut 1

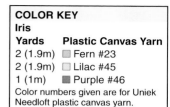

COLOR KEY
Iris

Yards	Plastic Canvas Yarn
2 (1.9m)	☐ Fern #23
2 (1.9m)	☐ Lilac #45
1 (1m)	■ Purple #46

Color numbers given are for Uniek
Needloft plastic canvas yarn.

Morning Glory

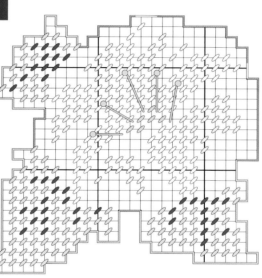

Morning Glory
25 holes x 25 holes
Cut 1

COLOR KEY
Morning Glory

Yards	Plastic Canvas Yarn
3 (2.8m)	☐ Moss #25
1 (1m)	■ Forest #29
1 (1m)	☐ Sail blue #35
2 (1.9m)	☐ White #41
1 (1m)	☐ Yellow #57
3 (2.8m)	Uncoded area are royal #32 Continental Stitches
	⁄ Royal #32 Overcasting
	⁄ Yellow #57 Straight Stitch
	○ Yellow #57 French Knot

Color numbers given are for Uniek Needloft
plastic canvas yarn.

Bright Flower

Bright Flower
17 holes x 17 holes
Cut 1

COLOR KEY
Bright Flower

Yards	Plastic Canvas Yarn
4 (3.7m)	☐ Bright pink #62
1 (1m)	☐ Bright yellow #63
1 (1m)	■ Bright purple #64
	⁄ Bright yellow #63 Straight Stitch

Color numbers given are for Uniek Needloft plastic
canvas yarn.

Strawberry Blossoms

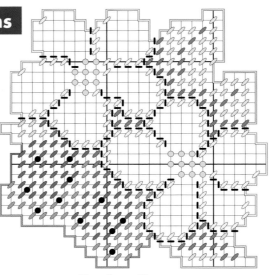

Strawberry Blossoms
25 holes x 25 holes
Cut 1

Pink Tulip

Pink Tulip
21 holes x 19 holes
Cut 1

Rose Blush

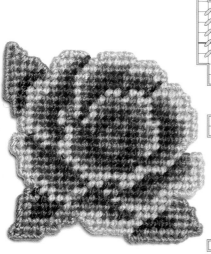

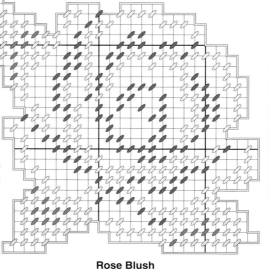

Rose Blush
25 holes x 25 holes
Cut 1

Watering Can Blossoms

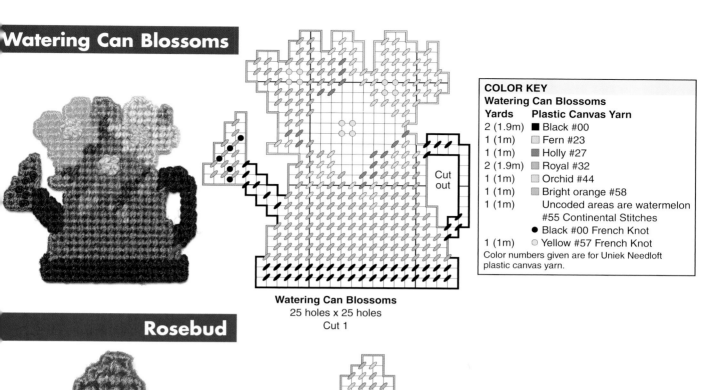

Cut out

Watering Can Blossoms
25 holes x 25 holes
Cut 1

Rosebud

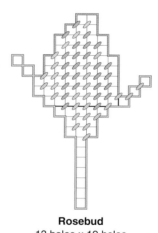

Rosebud
13 holes x 19 holes
Cut 1

Basket of Pansies

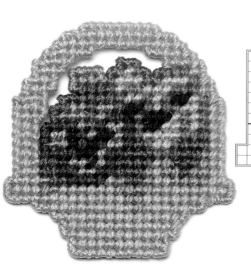

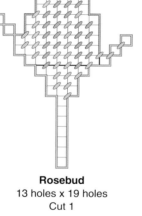

Cut out

Basket of Pansies
24 holes x 25 holes
Cut 1

Minis

These mini motifs add a bit of style to gifts and plants! Each of them can be stitched in just a few hours.

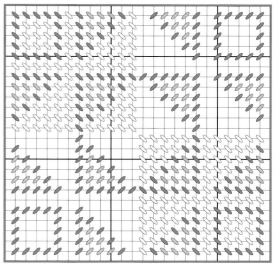

COLOR KEY
Southwest Square 1

Yards	Plastic Canvas Yarn
2 (1.9m)	▢ Rust #09
4 (3.7m)	◼ Holly #27
7 (6.5m)	▢ Eggshell #39

Uncoded areas are eggshell
#39 Continental Stitches
Color numbers given are for Uniek Needloft
plastic canvas yarn.

Southwest Square 1
25 holes x 25 holes
Cut 1

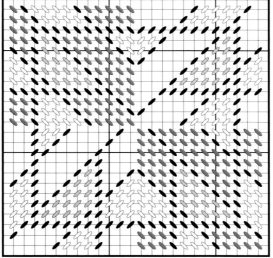

COLOR KEY
Southwest Square 2

Yards	Plastic Canvas Yarn
2 (1.9m)	◼ Black #00
7 (6.5m)	◼ Red #01
2 (1.9m)	▢ Silver #37
1 (1m)	▢ Gray #38

Uncoded areas are red
#01 Continental Stitches
Color numbers given are for Uniek Needloft
plastic canvas yarn.

Southwest Square 2
25 holes x 25 holes
Cut 1

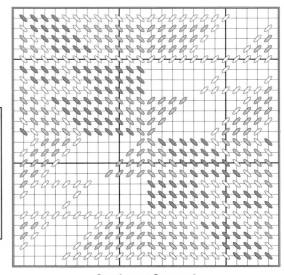

COLOR KEY
Southwest Square 3

Yards	Plastic Canvas Yarn
4 (3.7m)	▢ Maple #13
7 (6.5m)	◼ Brown #15
2 (1.9m)	▢ Beige #40

Uncoded areas are brown
#15 Continental Stitches
Color numbers given are for Uniek Needloft
plastic canvas yarn.

Southwest Square 3
25 holes x 25 holes
Cut 1

Southwestern Design

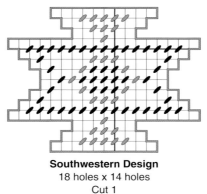

Southwestern Design
18 holes x 14 holes
Cut 1

COLOR KEY
Southwestern Design

Yards	Plastic Canvas Yarn
1 (1m)	■ Black #00
1 (1m)	■ Rust #09
2 (1.9m)	Uncoded areas are turquoise #54 Continental Stitches
	⁄ Turquoise #54 Overcasting

Color numbers given are for Uniek Needloft plastic canvas yarn.

Palm Branch

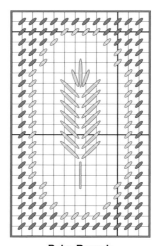

Palm Branch
13 holes x 22 holes
Cut 1

COLOR KEY
Palm Branch

Yards	Plastic Canvas Yarn
3 (2.8m)	■ Royal #32
3 (2.8m)	Uncoded background is white #41 Continental Stitches
	Metallic Craft Cord
2 (1.9m)	☐ Gold #55001
	⁄ Gold #55001 Straight Stitch

Color numbers given are for Uniek Needloft plastic canvas yarn and metallic craft cord.

The Sign of the Fish

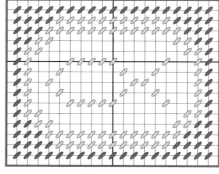

The Sign of the Fish
20 holes x 16 holes
Cut 1

COLOR KEY
The Sign of the Fish

Yards	Plastic Canvas Yarn
3 (2.8m)	■ Red #01
3 (2.8m)	Uncoded background is white #41 Continental Stitches
	Metallic Craft Cord
2 (1.9m)	☐ Gold #55001

Color numbers given are for Uniek Needloft plastic canvas yarn and metallic craft cord.

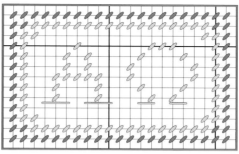

COLOR KEY
Alpha Omega

Yards	Plastic Canvas Yarn
3 (2.8m)	■ Royal #32
4 (3.7m)	Uncoded background is white #41 Continental Stitches
	Metallic Craft Cord
2 (1.9m)	☐ Gold #55001
	⁄ Gold #55001 Straight Stitch

Color numbers given are for Uniek Needloft plastic canvas yarn and metallic craft cord.

Alpha Omega
22 holes x 14 holes
Cut 1

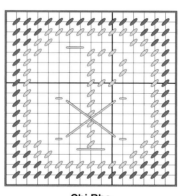

COLOR KEY
Chi Rho

Yards	Plastic Canvas Yarn
3 (2.8m)	■ Burgundy #03
2 (1.9m)	Uncoded background is white #41 Continental Stitches
	Metallic Craft Cord
3 (2.8m)	☐ Gold #55001
	⁄ Gold #55001 Straight Stitch

Color numbers given are for Uniek Needloft plastic canvas yarn and metallic craft cord.

Chi Rho
16 holes x 17 holes
Cut 1

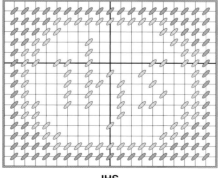

COLOR KEY
IHS

Yards	Plastic Canvas Yarn
3 (2.8m)	■ Purple #46
3 (2.8m)	Uncoded background is white #41 Continental Stitches
	Metallic Craft Cord
2 (1.9m)	☐ Gold #55001

Color numbers given are for Uniek Needloft plastic canvas yarn and metallic craft cord.

IHS
20 holes x 16 holes
Cut 1

Red, White & Blue Square 1

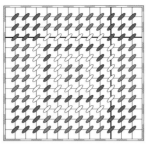

Red, White & Blue Square 1
13 holes x 13 holes
Cut 1

COLOR KEY
Red, White & Blue Square 1
Yards   Worsted Weight Yarn
1 (1m) ☐ Aran #313
1 (1m) ■ Cranberry #7074
1 (1m) ■ Stormy #7080
1 (1m) ✎ Linen #330 Overcasting
Color numbers given are for Coats &
Clark Red Heart Super Saver worsted
weight yarn Art. E300 and Tweed light
worsted weight yarn Art. E717.

Red, White & Blue Square 2

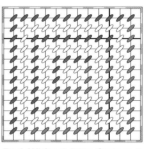

Red, White & Blue Square 2
13 holes x 13 holes
Cut 1

COLOR KEY
Red, White & Blue Square 2
Yards   Worsted Weight Yarn
1 (1m) ☐ Aran #313
1 (1m) ■ Cranberry #7074
1 (1m) ■ Stormy #7080
1 (1m) ✎ Linen #330 Overcasting
Color numbers given are for Coats &
Clark Red Heart Super Saver worsted
weight yarn Art. E300 and Tweed light
worsted weight yarn Art. E717.

Red, White & Blue Square 3

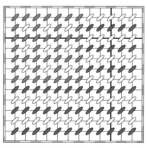

Red, White & Blue Square 3
13 holes x 13 holes
Cut 1

COLOR KEY
Red, White & Blue Square 3
Yards   Worsted Weight Yarn
1 (1m) ☐ Aran #313
1 (1m) ■ Cranberry #7074
1 (1m) ■ Stormy #7080
1 (1m) ✎ Linen #330 Overcasting
Color numbers given are for Coats &
Clark Red Heart Super Saver worsted
weight yarn Art. E300 and Tweed light
worsted weight yarn Art. E717.

Amish Square

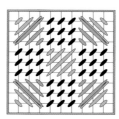

Amish Square
10 holes x 10 holes
Cut 1

COLOR KEY
Amish Square
Yards	Plastic Canvas Yarn
1 (1m)	■ Black #00
1 (1m)	▨ Purple #46
1 (1m)	▢ Turquoise #54
	╱ Turquoise #54 Straight Stitch

Color numbers given are for Uniek Needloft plastic canvas yarn.

Nine Patch

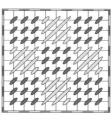

Nine Patch
10 holes x 10 holes
Cut 1

COLOR KEY
Nine Patch
Yards	Plastic Canvas Yarn
1 (1m)	■ Christmas red #02
1 (1m)	▢ Yellow #56

Color numbers given are for Uniek Needloft plastic canvas yarn.

Purple Quilt Block

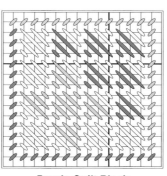

Purple Quilt Block
15 holes x 15 holes
Cut 1

COLOR KEY
Purple Quilt Block
Yards	Plastic Canvas Yarn
2 (1.9m)	▢ White #41
1 (1m)	▨ Lilac #45
1 (1m)	■ Purple #46

Color numbers given are for Uniek Needloft plastic canvas yarn.

Pink Quilt Block

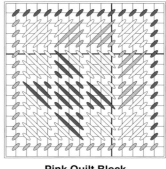

Pink Quilt Block
15 holes x 15 holes
Cut 1

Blue Quilt Block

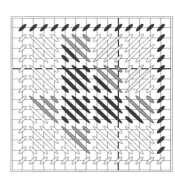

Blue Quilt Block
15 holes x 15 holes
Cut 1

Green Quilt Block

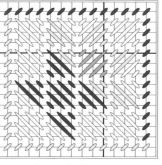

Green Quilt Block
15 holes x 15 holes
Cut 1

Log Cabin

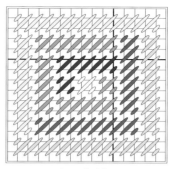

Log Cabin
15 holes x 15 holes
Cut 1

COLOR KEY
Log Cabin

Yards	Plastic Canvas Yarn
1 (1m)	■ Red #01
1 (1m)	■ Christmas red #02
1 (1m)	■ Royal #32
1 (1m)	□ Sail blue #35
1 (1m)	□ White #41
1 (1m)	■ Dark royal #48
1 (1m)	■ Watermelon #55

Color numbers given are for Uniek Needloft plastic canvas yarn.

Log Cabin Variation

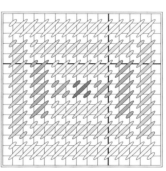

Log Cabin Variation
15 holes x 15 holes
Cut 1

COLOR KEY
Log Cabin Variation

Yards	Plastic Canvas Yarn
1 (1m)	□ Rust #09
1 (1m)	□ Tangerine #11
1 (1m)	■ Pumpkin #12
1 (1m)	■ Maple #13
1 (1m)	■ Brown #15
1 (1m)	□ Lemon #20
1 (1m)	■ Yellow #57

Color numbers given are for Uniek Needloft plastic canvas yarn.

Quilt Basket

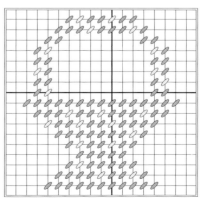

Quilt Basket
18 holes x 18 holes
Cut 1

COLOR KEY
Quilt Basket

Yards	Worsted Weight Yarn
1 (1m)	□ Rose pink #372
2 (1.9m)	■ Country rose #374
4 (3.7m)	Uncoded areas are eggnog #329 Continental Stitches
	╱ Eggnog #329 Overcasting

Color numbers given are for Coats & Clark Red Heart Super Saver worsted weight yarn Art. E300.

Quilt Heart

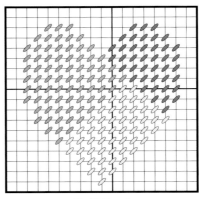

Quilt Heart
18 holes x 18 holes
Cut 1

COLOR KEY
Quilt Heart

Yards	Worsted Weight Yarn
2 (1.9m)	☐ Rose pink #372
2 (1.9m)	◼ Country rose #374
1 (1m)	☐ Denim heather #408
2 (1.9m)	◼ Medium sage #632
4 (3.7m)	Uncoded areas are cornmeal #220 Continental Stitches
	╱ Cornmeal #220 Overcasting

Color numbers given are for Coats & Clark Red Heart Classic worsted weight yarn Art. E267 and Super Saver worsted weight yarn Art. E300.

Quilt Star

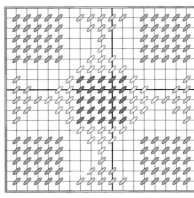

Quilt Star
18 holes x 18 holes
Cut 1

COLOR KEY
Quilt Star

Yards	Worsted Weight Yarn
1 (1m)	☐ Rose pink #372
4 (3.7m)	◼ Country rose #374
1 (1m)	☐ Light sage #631
1 (1m)	◼ Medium sage #632
3 (2.8m)	Uncoded areas are cornmeal #320 Continental Stitches

Color numbers given are for Coats & Clark Red Heart Super Saver worsted weight yarn Art. E300.

Quilt Bow

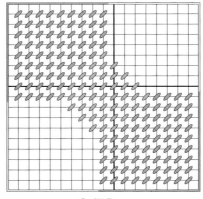

Quilt Bow
18 holes x 18 holes
Cut 1

COLOR KEY
Quilt Bow

Yards	Worsted Weight Yarn
5 (4.6m)	◼ Country rose #374
1 (1m)	☐ Denim heather #408
4 (3.7m)	Uncoded areas are cornmeal #220 Continental Stitches
	╱ Cornmeal #220 Overcasting

Color numbers given are for Coats & Clark Red Heart Classic worsted weight yarn Art. E267 and Super Saver worsted weight yarn Art. E300.

Babies

Need last minute baby shower favors? How about stitching one of these motifs for each shower guest as a lasting rememberance of the happy event!

Mini Birth Sampler

Mini Birth Sampler
24 holes x 24 holes
Cut 1

COLOR KEY
Mini Birth Sampler

Yards	Worsted Weight Yarn
1 (1m)	☐ White #1
2 (1.9m)	☐ Tan #334
1 (1m)	☐ Warm brown #336
1 (1m)	☐ Mist green #681
1 (1m)	☐ Pink #737
1 (1m)	☐ Blue jewel #818
5 (4.6m)	Uncoded background is maize #261 Continental Stitches
	✎ White #1 (2-ply) Straight Stitch
	✎ Mist green #681 Straight Stitch
	○ White #1 (4-ply) French Knot
	● Pink #737 (4-ply) French Knot
	● Blue jewel #818 (4-ply) French Knot

Heavy (#32) Braid

2 (1.9m)	✎ Confetti pink #032 Backstitch and Straight Stitch

#5 Pearl Cotton

4 (3.7m)	✎ Black (1-strand) Backstitch Straight Stitch
	✎ Black (4-strand) Straight Stitch
	☐ Center and stitch name in this area
	☐ Center and stitch date in this area

Color numbers given are for Coats & Clark Red Heart Classic worsted weight yarn Art. E267 and Kreinik Heavy (#32) Braid.

Mini Birth Sampler Alphabet
Stitch name and date on sampler
using these letters and numbers

Yellow Rattle

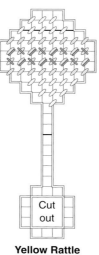

Cut out

Yellow Rattle
9 holes x 22 holes
Cut 1

COLOR KEY
Yellow Rattle

Yards	Plastic Canvas Yarn
1 (1m)	☐ Pink #07
1 (1m)	☐ Baby blue #36
2 (1.9m)	☐ Eggshell #39
	#3 Pearl Cotton
1 (1m)	✎ Pink Backstitch

Color numbers given are for Uniek Needloft plastic canvas yarn.

46

■ *401 Plastic Canvas Itty Bitties* ■

Tubby Duck

Tubby Duck
25 holes x 22 holes
Cut 1

COLOR KEY
Tubby Duck

Yards		Worsted Weight Yarn
3 (2.8m)	☐	White #1
1 (1m)	☐	Cornmeal #220
1 (1m)	▨	Pumpkin #254
1 (1m)	☐	Nickel #401
1 (1m)	■	Light lavender #579
1 (1m)	☐	Pale rose #755
1 (1m)	▨	Cameo rose #759
2 (1.9m)		Uncoded background on tub is pale blue #815 Continental Stitches
	⁄	Pale blue #815 Overcasting
	⁄	Cameo rose #759 (2-ply) Straight Stitch
	○	Cornmeal #220 (³/₈-inch/ 1cm-long) Lark s Head Knot

Medium (#16) Braid

1 (1m)	⁄	Pearl #032 Straight Stitch

#5 Pearl Cotton

2 (1.9m)	✎	Black (1-strand) Backstitch and Straight Stitch
	⁄	Black (4-strand) Straight Stitch

Color numbers given are for Coats & Clark Red Heart Classic worsted weight yarn Art. E267 and Kreinik Medium (#16) Braid.

Embroidered Bootee

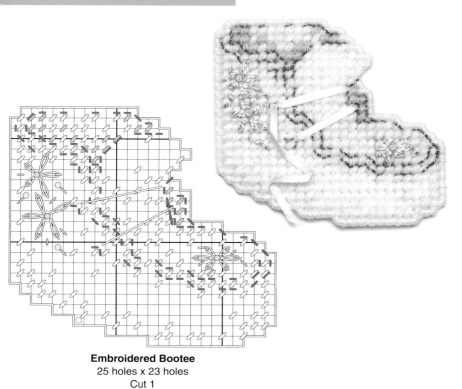

Embroidered Bootee
25 holes x 23 holes
Cut 1

COLOR KEY
Embroidered Bootee

Yards		Worsted Weight Yarn
4 (3.7m)	☐	Eggshell #111
1 (1m)	☐	Tan #334
4 (3.7m)		Uncoded background is off-white #3 Continental Stitches

#5 Pearl Cotton

2 (1.9m)	⁄	Medium beaver gray #647 Backstitch and Straight Stitch

#3 Pearl Cotton

1 (1m)	⁄	Very light pistachio green #369 Straight Stitch
1 (1m)	⊘	Ultra very light blue # 828 Lazy Daisy Stitch
1 (1m)	○	Very light topaz #727 (1-wrap) French Knot
1 (1m)	○	Baby pink #818 (2-wrap) French Knot

¹/₈-Inch/0.3cm-Wide Satin Ribbon

1 (1m)	⁄	Ivory Straight Stitch
	○	Drape and twist ivory ribbon from top to bottom dots; glue down at two places

Color numbers given are for Coats & Clark Red Heart Classic worsted weight yarn Art. E267 and DMC #5 and #3 pearl cotton.

Duck Pull Toy

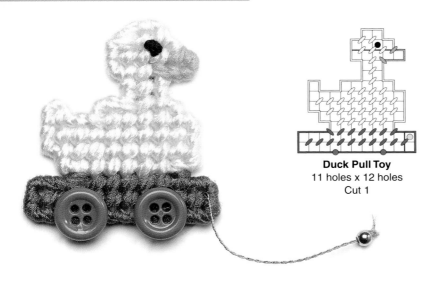

Duck Pull Toy
11 holes x 12 holes
Cut 1

Rocking Horse

Rocking Horse
24 holes x 24 holes
Cut 1

Cut out

Decorative Rattle

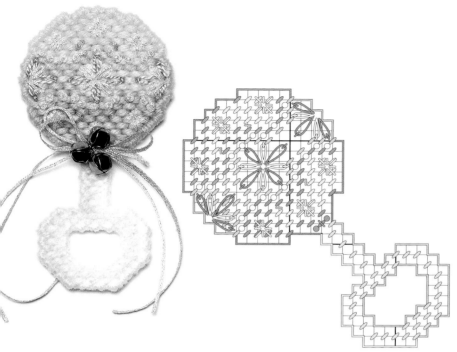

Decorative Rattle
25 holes x 25 holes
Cut 1

COLOR KEY
Decorative Rattle

Yards	Worsted Weight Yarn
2 (1.9m)	☐ White #1
1 (1m)	☐ Cornmeal #220
1 (1m)	☐ Lily pink #719
1 (1m)	☐ Pink #737
1 (1m)	☐ Pale blue #815
1 (1m)	☐ Blue jewel #818
1 (1m)	Uncoded areas are maize #261 Continental Stitches
	⟋ Maize #261 Overcasting

⅛-Inch Ribbon

1 (1m)	⟋ Star green #9194 Straight Stitch

Heavy (#32) Braid

3 (2.8m)	⟋ Pearl #032 Straight Stitch
	⟋ Pearl #032 Lazy Daisy Stitch
	○ Pearl #032 French Knot

#3 Pearl Cotton

1 (1m)	⟋ Light violet #554 Lazy Daisy Stitch
	● Attach bow (desired length each star green ribbon and pearl braid)
	⟍ Attach three ⅜-inch/9mm jingle bells over center of bow

Color numbers given are for Coats & Clark Red Heart Classic worsted weight yarn Art. E267, Kreinik ⅛-inch Ribbon and Heavy (#32) Braid and DMC #3 pearl cotton.

Golden Buggy

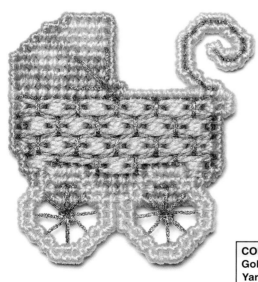

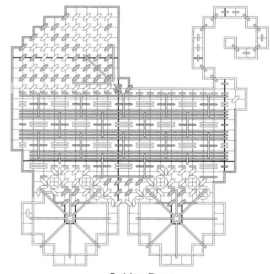

Golden Buggy
24 holes x 25 holes
Cut 1

COLOR KEY
Golden Buggy

Yards	Plastic Canvas Yarn
6 (5.5m)	☐ Eggshell #39
4 (3.7m)	☐ Beige #40
	⟋ Eggshell #39 Straight Stitch
	⟋ Beige #40 Straight Stitch
2 (1.9m)	⟋ Camel #43 Straight Stitch

Heavy (#32) Braid

3 (2.8m)	⟋ Gold #002 Backstitch and Straight Stitch

Color numbers given are for Uniek Needloft plastic canvas yarn and Kreinik Heavy (#32) Braid.

Hot Air Balloon

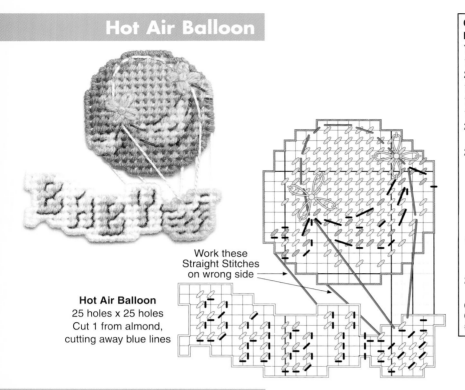

Hot Air Balloon
25 holes x 25 holes
Cut 1 from almond,
cutting away blue lines

Work these
Straight Stitches
on wrong side →

Pink Baby Carriage

Pink Baby Carriage
15 holes x 12 holes
Cut 1

Blue-Capped Baby Bottle

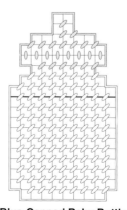

Blue-Capped Baby Bottle
10 holes x 18 holes
Cut 1

Teddy Bear Block

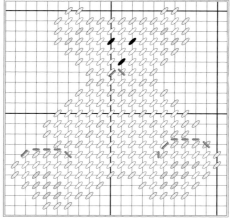

Teddy Bear Block
21 holes x 21 holes
Cut 1

COLOR KEY
Teddy Bear Block

Yards	Bulky Weight Yarn
4 (3.7m)	☐ Snowcap white #100
	Worsted Weight Yarn
1 (1m)	■ Black #312
3 (2.8m)	☐ Warm brown #336
1 (1m)	☐ Gray heather #400
4 (3.7m)	Uncoded areas are light mint #364 Continental Stitches
	⁄ Light mint #364 Overcasting
	6-Strand Embroidery Floss
1 (1m)	⁄ Black Backstitch

Color numbers given are for Lion Brand Chunky USA bulky weight yarn and Coats & Clark Red Heart Super Saver worsted weight yarn Art. E300.

Binky Bunny

COLOR KEY
Binky Bunny

Yards	Worsted Weight Yarn
1 (1m)	☐ White #1
3 (2.8m)	■ Warm brown #336
2 (1.9m)	☐ Lily pink #719
1 (1m)	■ Pink #737
1 (1m)	☐ Pale blue #815
3 (2.8m)	Uncoded areas are tan #334 Continental Stitches
	⁄ Pale blue #815 Backstitch
	#5 Pearl Cotton
3 (2.8m)	⁄ Black (1-strand) Backstitch and Straight Stitch
	⁄ Black (4-strand) Straight Stitch

Color numbers given are for Coats & Clark Red Heart Classic worsted weight yarn Art. E267.

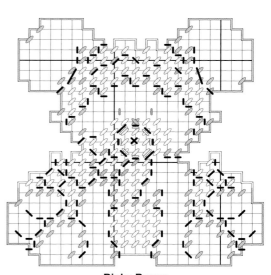

Binky Bunny
24 holes x 24 holes
Cut 1

Stuffed Teddy Bear

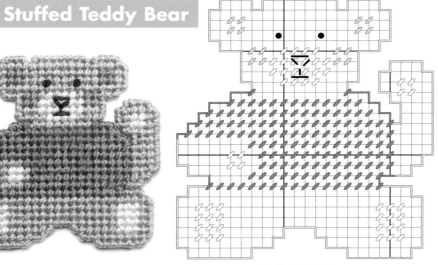

Stuffed Teddy Bear
24 holes x 25 holes
Cut 1

COLOR KEY
Stuffed Teddy Bear

Yards	Plastic Canvas Yarn
1 (1m)	■ Christmas red #02
3 (2.8m)	■ Royal #32
2 (1.9m)	☐ Eggshell #39
1 (1m)	☐ Watermelon #55
4 (3.7m)	Uncoded areas are sandstone #16 Continental Stitches
	⁄ Sandstone #16 Overcasting
1 (1m)	⁄ Black #00 Backstitch
	● Black #00 French Knot

Color numbers given are for Uniek Needloft plastic canvas yarn.

White-Capped Baby Bottle

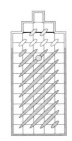

White-Capped Baby Bottle
5 holes x 12 holes
Cut 1

Baby With Bottle

Illustration on page 166

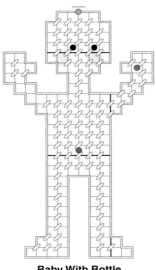

Baby With Bottle
14 holes x 24 holes
Cut 1

Baby in the Bathtub

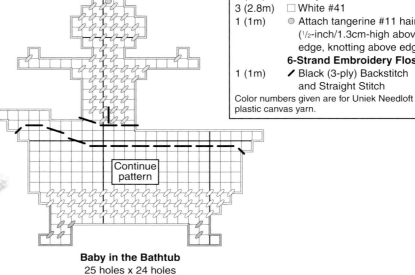

Continue pattern

Baby in the Bathtub
25 holes x 24 holes
Cut 1

Blue Baby Buggy

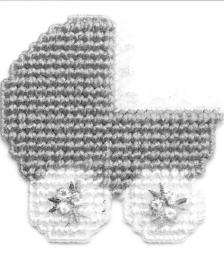

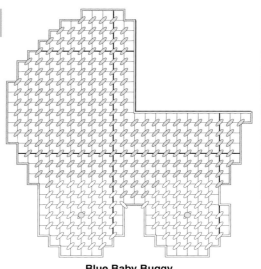

Blue Baby Buggy
23 holes x 24 holes
Cut 1

Hobby Horse

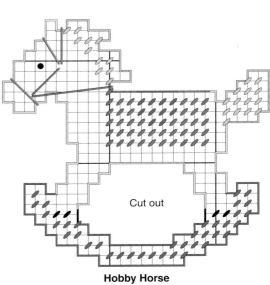

Cut out

Hobby Horse
25 holes x 24 holes
Cut 1

Golden Teddy

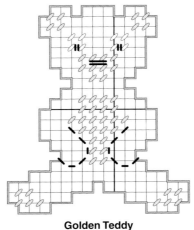

Golden Teddy
17 holes x 20 holes
Cut 1

Sunshine

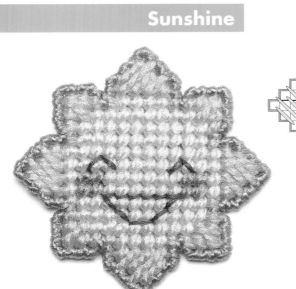

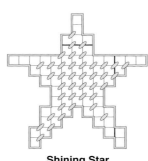

Sunshine
19 holes x 19 holes
Cut 1

COLOR KEY
Sunshine

Yards	Plastic Canvas Yarn
2 (1.9m)	☐ Tangerine #11
2 (1.9m)	☐ Pumpkin #12
2 (1.9m)	Uncoded background is yellow #57 Continental Stitches

6-Strand Embroidery Floss

1 (1m)	✎ Brown Backstitch

Color numbers given are for Uniek Needloft plastic canvas yarn.

Shining Star

Shining Star
13 holes x 13 holes
Cut 1

COLOR KEY
Shining Star

Yards	Plastic Canvas Yarn
2 (1.9m)	☐ Bright yellow #63

Color number given is for Uniek Needloft plastic canvas yarn.

Mini Clown

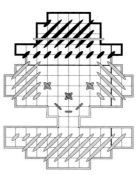

Mini Clown
12 holes x 15 holes
Cut 1

COLOR KEY
Mini Clown

Yards	Worsted Weight Yarn
1 (1m)	■ Black
1 (1m)	☐ Orange
1 (1m)	☐ Turquoise
1 (1m)	■ Dark brown
1 (1m)	■ Red
1 (1m)	Uncoded areas are peach Continental Stitches
	✎ Peach Overcasting
1 (1m)	✎ Yellow (2-ply) Straight Stitch
	✎ Red (1-ply) Backstitch

Smiley

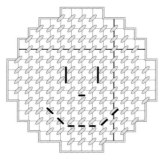

Smiley
14 holes x 14 holes
Cut 1

COLOR KEY
Smiley

Yards	Plastic Canvas Yarn
3 (2.8m)	☐ Yellow #57
	6-Strand Embroidery Floss
1 (1m)	✏ Black Backstitch and and Straight Stitch

Color number given is for Uniek Needloft plastic canvas yarn.

Baby Boy Star

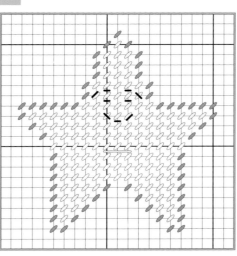

Baby Boy Star
22 holes x 23 holes
Cut 1

COLOR KEY
Baby Boy Star

Yards	Worsted Weight Yarn
1 (1m)	☐ White #311
2 (1.9m)	☐ Light blue #381
1 (1m)	■ Delft blue #885
7 (6.5m)	Uncoded areas are black #312 Continental Stitches
	✏ Black #312 Overcasting
	Metallic Craft Cord
1 (1m)	✏ White/silver #55008 Straight Stitch
	6-Strand Embroidery Floss
1 (1m)	✏ Black Backstitch and Straight Stitch

Color numbers given are for Coats & Clark Red Heart Super Saver worsted weight yarn Art. E300 and Uniek Needloft metallic craft cord.

Baby Girl Star

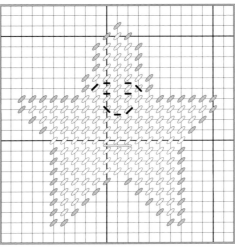

Baby Girl Star
22 holes x 23 holes
Cut 1

COLOR KEY
Baby Girl Star

Yards	Worsted Weight Yarn
1 (1m)	☐ White #311
2 (1.9m)	☐ Petal pink #373
1 (1m)	■ Light raspberry #774
7 (6.5m)	Uncoded areas are black #312 Continental Stitches
	✏ Black #312 Overcasting
	Metallic Craft Cord
1 (1m)	✏ White/silver #55008 Straight Stitch
	6-Strand Embroidery Floss
1 (1m)	✏ Black Backstitch and Straight Stitch

Color numbers given are for Coats & Clark Red Heart Super Saver worsted weight yarn Art. E300 and Uniek Needloft metallic craft cord.

Man in the Moon

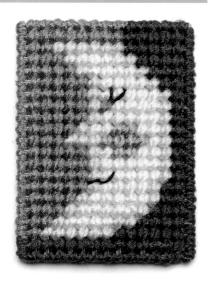

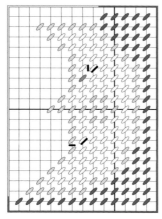

Man in the Moon
14 holes x 20 holes
Cut 1

COLOR KEY
Man in the Moon

Yards	Plastic Canvas Yarn
1 (1m)	Lavender #05
3 (2.8m)	Lemon #20
1 (1m)	Christmas green #28
4 (3.7m)	Dark royal #48
2 (1.9m)	Yellow #57
4 (3.7m)	Uncoded areas are royal #32 Continental Stitches
	Royal #32 Overcasting
	6-Strand Embroidery Floss
1 (1m)	Black Backstitch and Straight Stitch

Color numbers given are for Uniek Needloft plastic canvas yarn.

Yellow Star

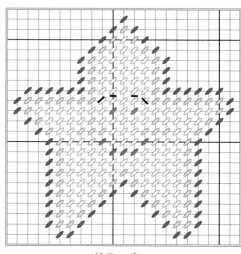

Yellow Star
22 holes 23 holes
Cut 1

COLOR KEY
Yellow Star

Yards	Plastic Canvas Yarn
1 (1m)	Red #01
1 (1m)	Lavender #05
4 (3.7m)	Lemon #20
1 (1m)	Christmas green #28
2 (1.9m)	Dark royal #48
2 (1.9m)	Yellow #57
7 (6.5m)	Uncoded areas are royal #32 Continental Stitches
	Royal #32 Overcasting
	6-Strand Embroidery Floss
1 (1m)	Black Backstitch and Straight Stitch

Color numbers given are for Uniek Needloft plastic canvas yarn.

Boys' Toys

Snips, snails and puppy dog tails are what little boys are made of, but so are cowboy boots, cars and trains! You'll find all sorts of motifs in this chapter suitable for little boy occasions!

Blue Pickup Truck

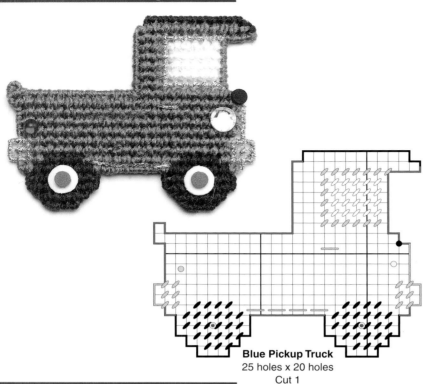

Blue Pickup Truck
25 holes x 20 holes
Cut 1

COLOR KEY
Blue Pickup Truck

Yards	Plastic Canvas Yarn
2 (1.9m)	■ Black #00
1 (1m)	☐ White #41
4 (3.7m)	Uncoded areas are royal #32 Continental Stitches
	╱ Royal #32 Overcasting

Solid Metallic Craft Cord

1 (1m)	▨ Solid silver #55021
	╱ Solid silver #55021 Backstitch and Straight Stitch
	○ Attach headlight (10mm round crystal faceted stone)
	◉ Attach taillight (5mm round ruby cabochon)
	● Attach hood ornament (1/4-inch/ 0.6cm black craft foam circle)
	⊛ Attach 12mm white craft foam circle under 6mm red craft foam circle

Color numbers given are for Uniek Needloft plastic canvas yarn.

Red Car

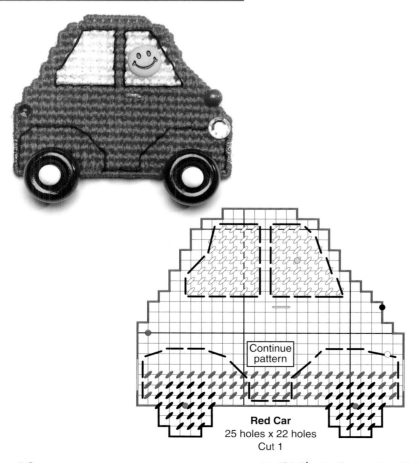

Continue pattern

Red Car
25 holes x 22 holes
Cut 1

COLOR KEY
Red Car

Yards	Plastic Canvas Yarn
2 (1.9m)	■ Christmas red #02
5 (4.6m)	☐ White #41

1/8-Inch Metallic Needlepoint Yarn

1 (1m)	╱ Silver #PC2 Straight Stitch and Overcasting

6-Strand Embroidery Floss

1 (1m)	╱ Black (3-ply) Backstitch
	○ Attach headlight (10mm round crystal faceted stone)
	● Attach taillight (7mm round ruby faceted stone)
	● Attach hood ornament (8mm round red cabochon)
	● Attach painted black tire (1-inch/2.5cm wooden wheel with 3/8-inch/0.5cm painted white wooden button hubcap)
	○ Attach smiling face bead or button

Color numbers given are for Uniek Needloft plastic canvas yarn and Rainbow Gallery Plastic Canvas 7 Metallic Needlepoint Yarn.

Ice-Cream Truck

COLOR KEY
Ice-Cream Truck

Yards	Plastic Canvas Yarn
2 (1.9m)	■ Black #00
1 (1m)	☐ Pink #07
1 (1m)	▨ Maple #13
1 (1m)	☐ Sail blue #35
1 (1m)	▨ Gray #38
1 (1m)	☐ Yellow #57
7 (6.5m)	Uncoded background is white #41 Continental Stitches
1 (1m)	∕ Christmas red #02 Overcasting
	∕ White #41 Overcasting

#3 Pearl Cotton

1 (1m)	∕ Black Backstitch
	Attach words "ice cream" (¼-inch/0.6cm-high sticker letters)
	↘ Attach American flag toothpick
	● Attach headlight (10mm round crystal faceted stone)
	● Attach taillight (7mm round ruby faceted stone)
	● Attach hood ornament (¼-inch/0.6cm black craft foam circle)

Color numbers given are for Uniek Needloft plastic canvas yarn.

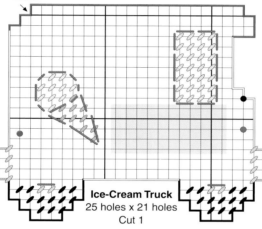

Ice-Cream Truck
25 holes x 21 holes
Cut 1

Red Boat

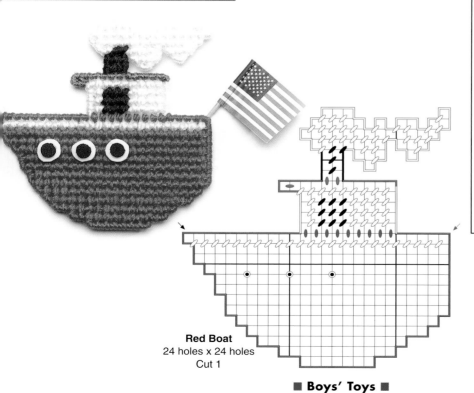

COLOR KEY
Red Boat

Yards	Plastic Canvas Yarn
1 (1m)	■ Black #00
5 (4.6m)	■ Christmas red #02
1 (1m)	▨ Royal #032
2 (1.9m)	☐ White #41
	Uncoded areas are Christmas red #02 Continental Stitches
	◉ Attach porthole (10mm white craft foam circle under 6mm black craft foam circle)
	∕ Attach American flag toothpick
	↘ Attach pole (⅞-inch/2.2cm-long round toothpick with 5mm gold bead glued to top end)

Color numbers given are for Uniek Needloft plastic canvas yarn.

Red Boat
24 holes x 24 holes
Cut 1

Screwdriver

Screwdriver
8 holes x 23 holes
Cut 1

COLOR KEY
Screwdriver

Yards	Worsted Weight Yarn
1 (1m)	☐ Orange #245
1 (1m)	☐ Cherry red #319
1 (1m)	■ Skipper blue #848
1 (1m)	■ Hot red #390
3 (2.8m)	Uncoded areas are white #311 Continental Stitches
	⁄ White #311 Overcasting

Color numbers given are for Coats & Clark Red Heart Classic worsted weight yarn Art. E267 and Super Saver worsted weight yarn Art. E300.

Pliers

Pliers
12 holes x 22 holes
Cut 1

COLOR KEY
Pliers

Yards	Worsted Weight Yarn
1 (1m)	■ Cherry red #319
1 (1m)	■ Paddy green #368
1 (1m)	■ Hot red #390
1 (1m)	☐ Emerald green #676
1 (1m)	■ Skipper blue #848
4 (3.7m)	☐ Uncoded areas are white #311 Continental Stitches
	⁄ White #311 Overcasting

Color numbers given are for Coats & Clark Red Heart Classic worsted weight yarn Art. E267 and Super Saver worsted weight yarn Art. E300.

Hammer

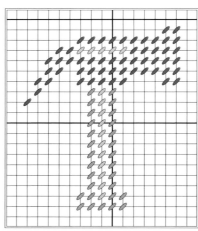

Hammer
18 holes x 21 holes
Cut 1

COLOR KEY
Hammer

Yards	Worsted Weight Yarn
1 (1m)	☐ Orange #245
1 (1m)	■ Cherry red #319
1 (1m)	☐ Vibrant orange #354
1 (1m)	■ Paddy green #368
1 (1m)	☐ Emerald green #676
1 (1m)	■ Skipper blue #848
7 (6.5m)	☐ Uncoded areas are white #311 Continental Stitches
	⁄ White #311 Overcasting

Color numbers given are for Coats & Clark Red Heart Classic worsted weight yarn Art. E267 and Super Saver worsted weight yarn Art. E300.

Red & Blue Crayons

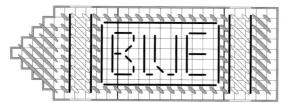

Blue Crayon
25 holes x 9 holes
Cut 1

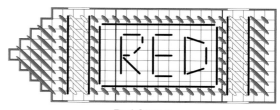

Red Crayon
25 holes x 9 holes
Cut 1

School Bus

School Bus Steering Wheel
Cut 1 from
black craft foam

School Bus
25 holes x 24 holes
Cut 1

Moon Man

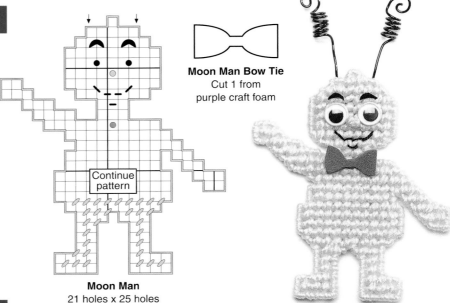

Moon Man Bow Tie
Cut 1 from purple craft foam

Continue pattern

Moon Man
21 holes x 25 holes
Cut 1

Jack-in-the-Box

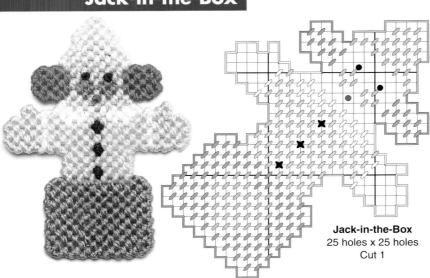

Jack-in-the-Box
25 holes x 25 holes
Cut 1

Cheerful Clown

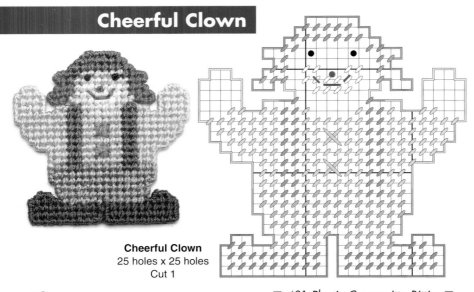

Cheerful Clown
25 holes x 25 holes
Cut 1

Clarence the Clown

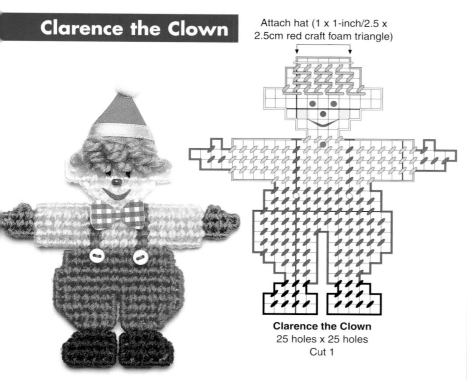

Attach hat (1 x 1-inch/2.5 x 2.5cm red craft foam triangle)

Clarence the Clown
25 holes x 25 holes
Cut 1

Taxi

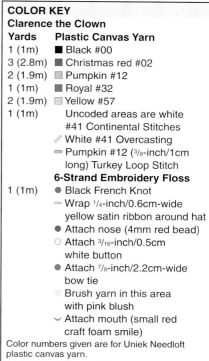

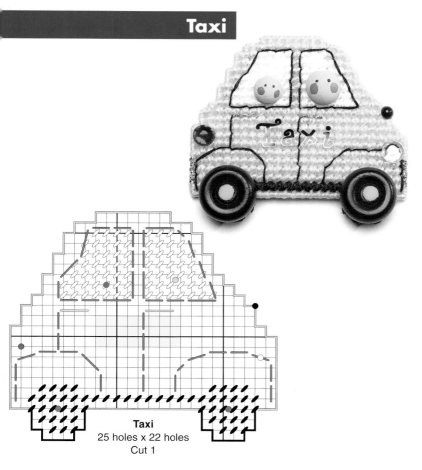

Taxi
25 holes x 22 holes
Cut 1

Brown Cowboy Boots

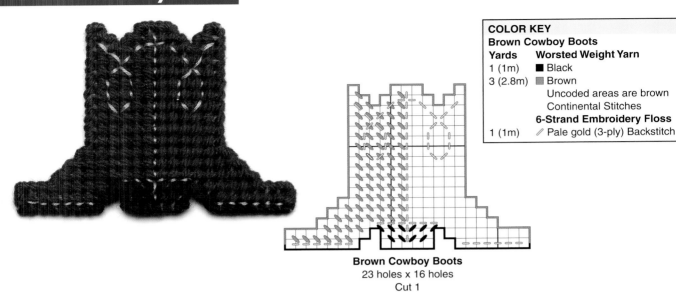

COLOR KEY
Brown Cowboy Boots

Yards	Worsted Weight Yarn
1 (1m)	■ Black
3 (2.8m)	■ Brown
	Uncoded areas are brown Continental Stitches

6-Strand Embroidery Floss

1 (1m)	⁄ Pale gold (3-ply) Backstitch

Brown Cowboy Boots
23 holes x 16 holes
Cut 1

Cow Skull

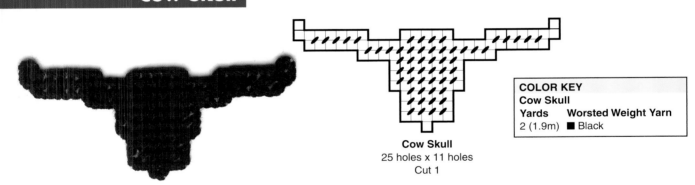

Cow Skull
25 holes x 11 holes
Cut 1

COLOR KEY
Cow Skull

Yards	Worsted Weight Yarn
2 (1.9m)	■ Black

Cowboy Hat

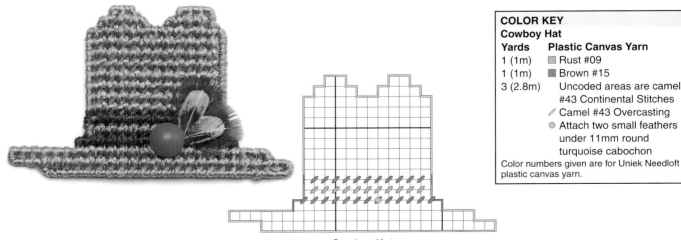

COLOR KEY
Cowboy Hat

Yards	Plastic Canvas Yarn
1 (1m)	▨ Rust #09
1 (1m)	▨ Brown #15
3 (2.8m)	Uncoded areas are camel #43 Continental Stitches
	⁄ Camel #43 Overcasting
	● Attach two small feathers under 11mm round turquoise cabochon

Color numbers given are for Uniek Needloft plastic canvas yarn.

Cowboy Hat
25 holes x 15 holes
Cut 1

Country Guitar

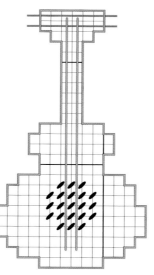

Country Guitar
14 holes x 25 holes
Cut 1

Country Guitar Tuning Pegs
Make 2 with
20-gauge black craft wire

Western Vest

Illustrations on page 166

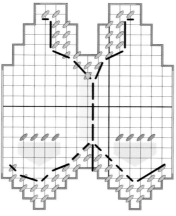

Western Vest
16 holes x 20 holes
Cut 1

Camel Cowboy Boot

Illustration on page 167

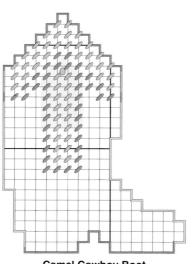

Camel Cowboy Boot
17 holes x 23 holes
Cut 1

Traffic Light

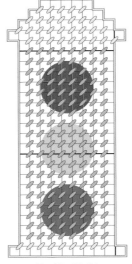

Traffic Light
11 holes x 25 holes
Cut 1

Go Sign

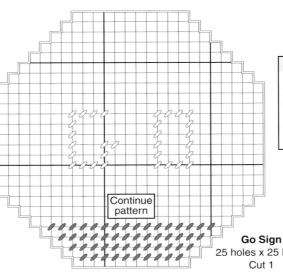

Continue pattern

Go Sign
25 holes x 25 holes
Cut 1

Stop Sign

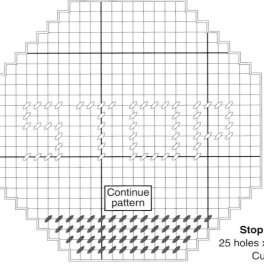

Continue pattern

Stop Sign
25 holes x 25 holes
Cut 1

Work Boot

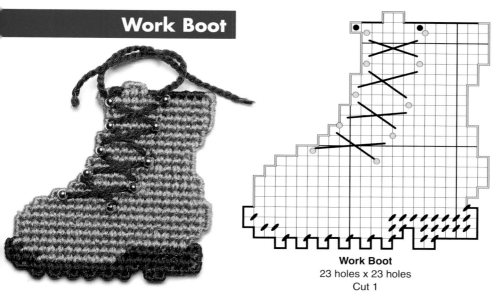

Work Boot
23 holes x 23 holes
Cut 1

COLOR KEY
Work Boot

Yards	Plastic Canvas Yarn
1 (1m)	■ Black #00
5 (4.6m)	Uncoded area is camel #43 Continental Stitches
	∕ Camel #43 Overcasting
	✕ Black #00 Cross Stitch
	● Attach shoelace tails (3½-inch/8.9cm-long Black #00)
	○ Attach 5mm gold bead

Color numbers given are for Uniek Needloft plastic canvas yarn.

Dump Truck

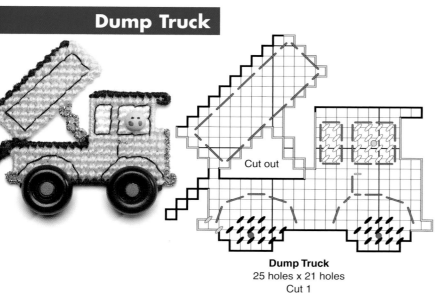

Dump Truck
25 holes x 21 holes
Cut 1

Cut out

COLOR KEY
Dump Truck

Yards	Plastic Canvas Yarn
2 (1.9m)	■ Black #00
1 (1m)	☐ White #41
4 (3.7m)	Uncoded areas are yellow #57 Continental Stitches
	∕ Yellow #57 Overcasting

⅛-Inch Metallic Needlepoint Yarn

1 (1m)	☐ Silver #PC2
	∕ Silver #PC2 Straight Stitch

6-Strand Embroidery Floss

1 (1m)	∕ Black (2-ply) Backstitch
	● Attach painted black tire (1-inch/2.5cm wooden wheel with ¼-inch/0.6cm red craft foam circle hubcap)
	○ Attach painted head (⅜-inch/10mm split wooden bead)

Color numbers given are for Uniek Needloft plastic canvas yarn and Rainbow Gallery Plastic Canvas 7 Metallic Needlepoint Yarn.

Bulldozer

Illustration on page 167

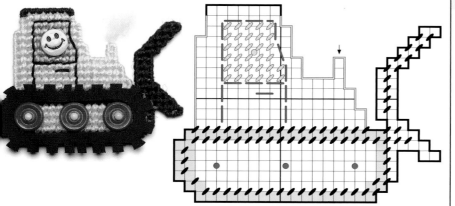

Bulldozer
25 holes x 19 holes
Cut 1

COLOR KEY
Bulldozer

Yards	Plastic Canvas Yarn
4 (3.7m)	■ Black #00
1 (1m)	☐ Bright blue #60
5 (4.6m)	Uncoded background is yellow #57 Continental Stitches
	∕ Yellow #57 Overcasting

6-Strand Embroidery Floss

1 (1m)	∕ Black Backstitch and Straight Stitch
	○ Attach smiling face bead or button
	☐ Attach traction tire (see pattern)
	● Attach painted red wheel (⅝-inch/1.6cm wooden wheel with yellow pin head or 4mm yellow bead in center)
	↓ Attach steam (small amount fiberfill)

Color numbers given are for Uniek Needloft plastic canvas yarn.

Train Engine

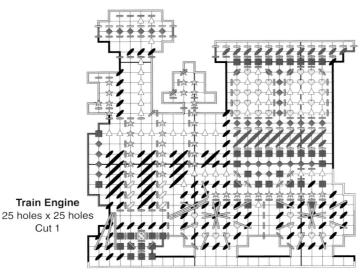

Train Engine
25 holes x 25 holes
Cut 1

Mini Train Locomotive

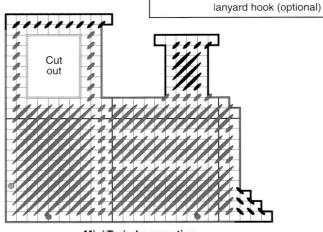

Mini Train Locomotive
25 holes x 20 holes
Cut 1

Mini Train Coal Car

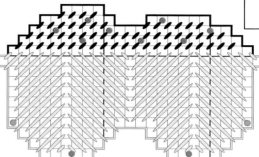

Mini Train Coal Car
25 holes x 15 holes
Cut 1

Mini Train Passenger Car

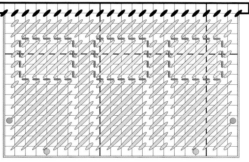

Mini Train Passenger Car
24 holes x 15 holes
Cut 1

Mini Train Caboose

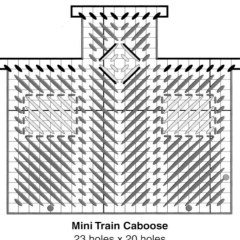

Mini Train Caboose
23 holes x 20 holes
Cut 1

Fire Engine

COLOR KEY
Fire Engine

Yards	Plastic Canvas Yarn
2 (1.9m)	■ Black #00
1 (1m)	☐ White #41
3 (2.8m)	Uncoded areas are Christmas red #02 Continental Stitches
	╱ Christmas red #02 Overcasting

⅛-Inch Metallic Needlepoint Yarn

1 (1m)	☐ Silver #PC2
	╱ Silver #PC2 Straight Stitch

6-Strand Embroidery Floss

1 (1m)	╱ Black (6-ply) Straight Stitch
	╱ Black (12-ply) Backstitch and Straight Stitch
	○ Attach headlight (10mm round crystal faceted stone)
	● Attach painted head (½-inch/13mm split wooden bead)
	● Attach painted black tire (1-inch/2.5cm wooden wheel with ¼-inch/0.6cm silver paper circle hubcap)
	● Attach ladder (see pattern)
	○ Attach fire hose (black rattail cord)
	↘ Attach hat (see pattern) to head and window

Color numbers given are for Uniek Needloft plastic canvas yarn and Rainbow Gallery Plastic Canvas 7 Metallic Needlepoint Yarn.

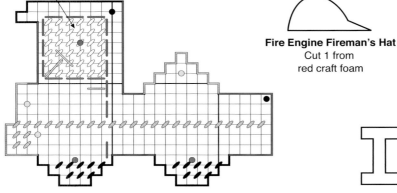

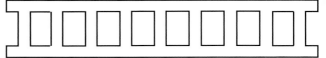

Fire Engine Fireman's Hat
Cut 1 from
red craft foam

Fire Engine
25 holes x 18 holes
Cut 1

Fire Engine Ladder
Cut 1 from
black craft foam

Fire Hydrant

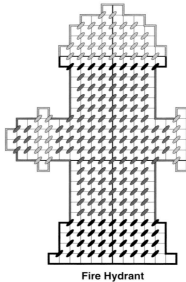

COLOR KEY
Fire Hydrant

Yards	Plastic Canvas Yarn
2 (1.9m)	■ Black #00
4 (3.7m)	■ Red #01
	Solid Metallic Craft Cord
2 (1.9m)	☐ Solid silver #55021

Color numbers given are for Uniek Needloft plastic canvas yarn and solid metallic craft cord.

Fire Hydrant
17 holes x 25 holes
Cut 1

Fireman's Hat

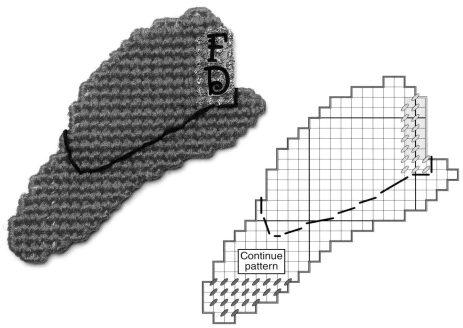

Fireman's Hat
24 holes x 24 holes
Cut 1

COLOR KEY
Fireman's Hat

Yards	Plastic Canvas Yarn
4 (3.7m)	■ Christmas red #02
	Solid Metallic Craft Cord
1 (1m)	□ Solid gold #55020
	6-Strand Embroidery Floss
1 (1m)	✏ Black Backstitch
	▢ Attach letters "F" and "D" (⁷⁄₁₆-inch/1.1cm-high sticker letters)

Color numbers given are for Uniek Needloft plastic canvas yarn and solid metallic craft cord.

Police Car

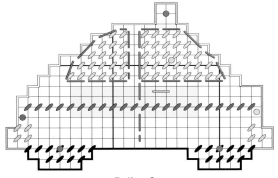

Police Car
25 holes x 16 holes
Cut 1

COLOR KEY
Police Car

Yards	Plastic Canvas Yarn
1 (1m)	■ Black #00
1 (1m)	■ Christmas red #02
2 (1.9m)	□ Bright blue #60
4 (3.7m)	Uncoded areas are white #41 Continental Stitches
	✏ White #41 Overcasting
	Solid Metallic Craft Cord
1 (1m)	□ Solid silver #55021
	✏ Solid silver #55021 Straight Stitch
	6-Strand Embroidery Floss
1 (1m)	✏ Black (2-ply) Backstitch
	○ Attach headlight (10mm round crystal faceted stone)
	● Attach taillight (6mm round ruby faceted stone)
	● Attach police light (8mm round dark sapphire cabochon)
	○ Attach painted head (¹⁄₂-inch/13mm split wooden bead)
	● Attach painted black tire (³⁄₄-inch/ 1.9cm wooden wheel with ¹⁄₄-inch/ 0.6cm red craft foam circle hubcap)
	▢ Attach word "Police" (¹⁄₄ to ¹⁄₂-inch/ 0.6 to 1.3cm-high sticker letters)

Color numbers given are for Uniek Needloft plastic canvas yarn and solid metallic craft cord.

Primary Colors Kite

Primary Colors Kite
15 holes x 22 holes
Cut 1

COLOR KEY
Primary Colors Kite

Yards	Plastic Canvas Yarn
1 (1m)	■ Red #01
2 (1.9m)	■ Christmas green #28
2 (1.9m)	■ Royal #32
1 (1m)	□ Yellow #57

¹/₄-Inch/0.6cm-Wide Satin Ribbon
○ Attach two yellow tails (each 13 inches/33cm long)
● Attach two red tails (each 13 inches/33cm long)

Color numbers given are for Uniek Needloft plastic canvas yarn.

Pink & Purple Kite

Pink & Purple Kite
23 holes x 12 holes
Cut 1

COLOR KEY
Pink & Purple Kite

Yards	Plastic Canvas Yarn
2 (1.9m)	■ Bright pink #62
1 (1m)	■ Bright purple #64

¹/₄-Inch/0.6cm-Wide Satin Ribbon
● Attach purple tail (8 inches/20.3cm)

Color numbers given are for Uniek Needloft plastic canvas yarn.

Kite

Kite
13 holes x 19 holes
Cut 1

COLOR KEY
Kite

Yards	Plastic Canvas Yarn
1 (1m)	■ Fern #23
1 (1m)	□ Lilac #45
1 (1m)	■ Turquoise #54
1 (1m)	■ Watermelon #55
1 (1m)	⟋ Tangerine #11 Overcasting
	○ Attach tail (6-inch/15.2cm length tangerine #11)

Color numbers given are for Uniek Needloft plastic canvas yarn.

Sport Shirt

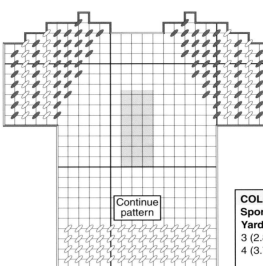

Continue pattern

Sport Shirt
25 holes x 25 holes
Cut 1

COLOR KEY
Sport Shirt

Yards	Plastic Canvas Yarn
3 (2.8m)	■ Christmas red #02
4 (3.7m)	☐ White #41
	▨ Attach 1¼-inch/3.2cm-high red craft foam "1"

Color numbers given are for Uniek Needloft plastic canvas yarn.

Baseball & Bat

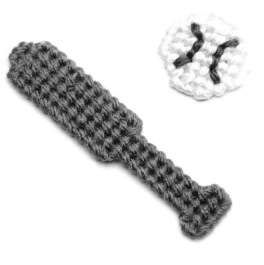

Baseball
7 holes x 7 holes
Cut 1

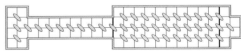

Bat
22 holes x 4 holes
Cut 1

COLOR KEY
Baseball & Bat

Yards	Worsted Weight Yarn
2 (1.9m)	▨ Taupe
1 (1m)	☐ White
1 (1m)	✏ Red Backstitch

Little Red Wagon

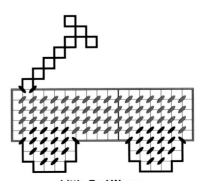

Little Red Wagon
17 holes x 15 holes
Cut 1

COLOR KEY
Little Red Wagon

Yards	Plastic Canvas Yarn
2 (1.9m)	■ Black #00
2 (1.9m)	▨ Red #01

Color numbers given are for Uniek Needloft plastic canvas yarn.

Girls, Girls, Girls

Girls just want to have fun! From pretty purses to whimsical fairies, these little motifs are full of fun and fancy.

Dollhouse

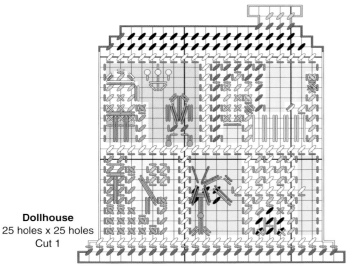

Dollhouse
25 holes x 25 holes
Cut 1

COLOR KEY
Dollhouse

Yards	Plastic Canvas Yarn
3 (2.8m)	☐ Off-white #3
1 (1m)	■ Black #12
1 (1m)	☐ Cornmeal #220
1 (1m)	▨ Mid brown #339
1 (1m)	☐ Silver #412
2 (1.9m)	▨ Claret #762
	Uncoded background in yellow shaded area is cornmeal #220 Continental Stitches
2 (1.9m)	Uncoded backgrounds in green shaded areas are light sage #631 Continental Stitches
1 (1m)	Uncoded backgrounds in pink shaded areas are cameo rose #759 Continental Stitches
2 (1.9m)	Uncoded backgrounds in blue shaded areas are country blue #882 Continental Stitches
	╱ Off-white #3 (2-ply) Straight Stitch
	╱ Cornmeal #220 (4-ply) Straight Stitch
	╱ Light sage #631 (2-ply) Straight Stitch
1 (1m)	╱ Dark sage #633 (1-ply) combined with light sage #631 (1-ply) Straight Stitch
	○ Cornmeal #220 (2-ply/2-wrap) French Knot

Medium #16 Braid

2 (1.9m)	▨ Gold #002 (4 strands)
	╱ Gold #002 (1 strand) Backstitch, Straight Stitch and Cross Stitch

#3 Pearl Cotton

3 (2.8m)	▨ Dark golden brown #975 (2 strands)
	╱ Dark golden brown #975 (1 strand) Backstitch and Straight Stitch
	● Dark golden brown #975 (1 strand) French Knot

#5 Pearl Cotton

4 (3.7m)	╱ Black #310 (1 strand) Backstitch and Straight Stitch
2 (1.9m)	╱ Ultra dark beaver gray #844 (1 strand) Backstitch

Color numbers given are for Coats & Clark Red Heart Classic worsted weight yarn Art. E267, Kreinik Medium (#16) Braid and DMC #3 and #5 pearl cotton.

Framed Purse

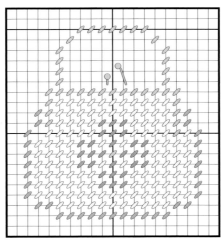

Framed Purse
20 holes x 22 holes
Cut 1

COLOR KEY
Framed Purse

Yards	Plastic Canvas Yarn
4 (3.7m)	☐ Eggshell #39
2 (1.9m)	▨ Camel #43
1 (1m)	▨ Watermelon #55
5 (4.6m)	Uncoded background is black #00 Continental Stitches Black #00 Overcasting

Metallic Craft Cord

2 (1.9m)	▨ Gold #55001
	╱ Gold #55001 Backstitch
	● Gold #55001 French Knot

Color numbers given are for Uniek Needloft plastic canvas yarn and metallic craft cord.

Dancing Frog

Dancing Frog
24 holes x 24 holes
Cut 1

Continue pattern

Ballet Slippers

Illustration on page 167

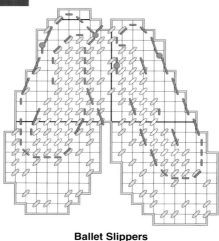

Ballet Slippers
20 holes x 21 holes
Cut 1

Ballerina

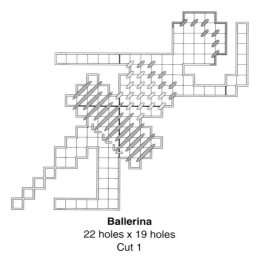

Ballerina
22 holes x 19 holes
Cut 1

Bunnymobile

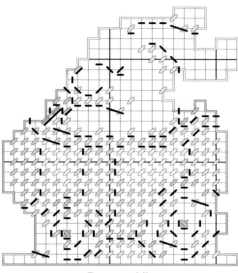

Bunnymobile
22 holes x 25 holes
Cut 1

COLOR KEY		
Bunnymobile		
Yards	**Plastic Canvas Yarn**	
1 (1m)	☐ Pink #07	
1 (1m)	☐ Baby yellow #21	
2 (1.9)	☐ Fern #23	
1 (1m)	☐ Sail blue #35	
1 (1m)	☐ Silver #37	
1 (1m)	☐ Lilac #45	
2 (1.9m)	☐ Yellow #57	
3 (2.8m)	Uncoded areas are white #41 Continental Stitches	
	╱ White #41 Overcasting	
	╱ Fern #23 Straight Stitch	
#5 Pearl Cotton		
3 (2.8m)	╱ Black Backstitch and Straight Stitch	

Color numbers given are for Uniek Needloft plastic canvas yarn.

Balloon Bear

Balloon Bear
25 holes x 25 holes
Cut 1

COLOR KEY		
Balloon Bear		
Yards	**Worsted Weight Yarn**	
1 (1m)	☐ White #1	
1 (1m)	■ Black #12	
1 (1m)	☐ Eggshell #111	
2 (1.9m)	☐ Maize #261	
1 (1m)	☐ Warm brown #336	
2 (1.9m)	■ Country red #914	
3 (2.8m)	Uncoded areas are tan #334 Continental Stitches	
	╱ White #1 Backstitch and Straight Stitch	
	╱ Maize #261 Straight Stitch	
	● Attach white #1 bow	
Heavy (#32) Braid		
5 (4.6m)	☐ Star yellow #091	
#5 Pearl Cotton		
2 (1.9m)	╱ Black Backstitch and Straight Stitch	
	↘ Attach string (14 inches/ 35.6cm 30-gauge white covered stem wire) (see general instructions)	

Color numbers given are for Coats & Clark Red Heart Classic worsted weight yarn Art. E267 and Kreinik Heavy (#32) Braid.

Blue Willow Teapot

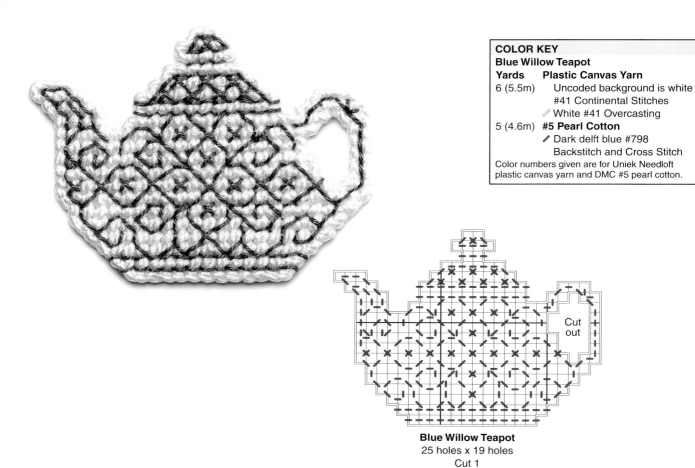

Cut out

Blue Willow Teapot
25 holes x 19 holes
Cut 1

Blue Willow Teacup

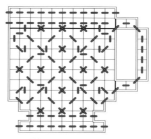

Blue Willow Teacup
13 holes x 12 holes
Cut 1

Blue Willow Saucer

Blue Willow Saucer
14 holes x 14 holes
Cut 1

COLOR KEY
Blue Willow Saucer

Yards	Plastic Canvas Yarn
3 (2.8m)	Uncoded background is white #41 Continental Stitches
	⟋ White #41 Overcasting
3 (2.8m)	**#5 Pearl Cotton**
	⟋ Dark delft blue #798 Backstitch and Cross Stitch

Color numbers given are for Uniek Needloft plastic canvas yarn and DMC #5 pearl cotton.

Blue Willow Creamer

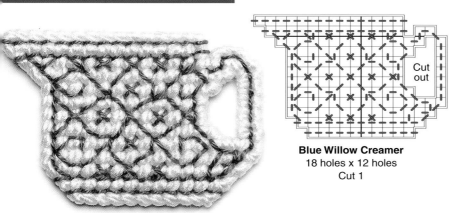

Blue Willow Creamer
18 holes x 12 holes
Cut 1

COLOR KEY
Blue Willow Creamer

Yards	Plastic Canvas Yarn
3 (2.8m)	Uncoded background is white #41 Continental Stitches
	⟋ White #41 Overcasting
3 (2.8m)	**#5 Pearl Cotton**
	⟋ Dark delft blue #798 Backstitch and Cross Stitch

Color numbers given are for Uniek Needloft plastic canvas yarn and DMC #5 pearl cotton.

lue Willow Sugar Bowl

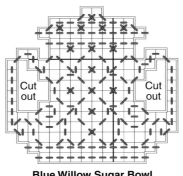

Blue Willow Sugar Bowl
16 holes x 15 holes
Cut 1

COLOR KEY
Blue Willow Sugar Bowl

Yards	Plastic Canvas Yarn
5 (4.6m)	Uncoded background is white #41 Continental Stitches
	⟋ White #41 Overcasting
	#5 Pearl Cotton
4 (3.7m)	⟋ Dark delft blue #798 Backstitch and Cross Stitch

Color numbers given are for Uniek Needloft plastic canvas yarn and DMC #5 pearl cotton.

Glowing Star

Glowing Star
25 holes x 25 holes
Cut 1

Bunny in Blue Jumper

 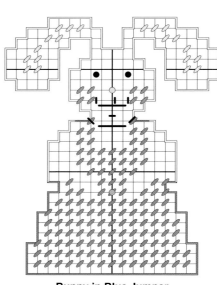

Bunny in Blue Jumper
20 holes x 25 holes
Cut 1

Unicorn

 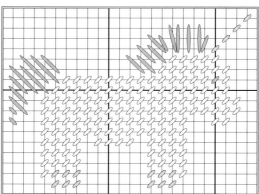

Unicorn
24 holes x 18 holes
Cut 1

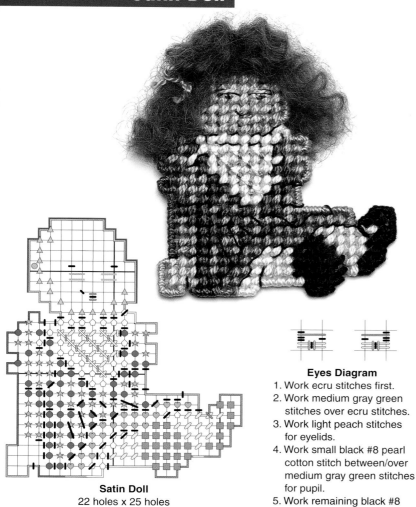

COLOR KEY
Satin Doll

Yards	#3 Pearl Cotton (2 strands)
2 (1.9m)	○ White
2 (1.9m)	⊘ Ecru
2 (1.9m)	♥ Light shell pink #223
2 (1.9m)	■ Black #310
2 (1.9m)	△ Very light terra-cotta #758
3 (2.8m)	● Dark green gray #3051
3 (2.8m)	☆ Green gray #3053
2 (1.9m)	Uncoded areas are light peach #754 Continental Stitches
	∕ White (1 strand) Straight Stitch
	∕ Ecru (1 strand) Straight Stitch
	∕ Light shell pink #223 (1-strand) Straight Stitch
	∕ Black #310 (1-strand) Straight Stitch
	∕ Light peach #754 (1-strand) Straight Stitch
1 (1m)	∕ Medium gray green #926 (1-strand) Straight Stitch
	● Attach small green gray #3053 bow

#8 Pearl Cotton

3 (2.8m)	∕ Black (1-strand) Backstitch and Straight Stitch
	− Attach hair (4-inch/10.1cm-length light brown curly crepe wool hair
	═ Eye placement (see eyes diagram)

Color numbers given are for DMC #3 pearl cotton.

Eyes Diagram

1. Work ecru stitches first.
2. Work medium gray green stitches over ecru stitches.
3. Work light peach stitches for eyelids.
4. Work small black #8 pearl cotton stitch between/over medium gray green stitches for pupil.
5. Work remaining black #8 pearl cotton stitches.

Satin Doll
22 holes x 25 holes
Cut 1

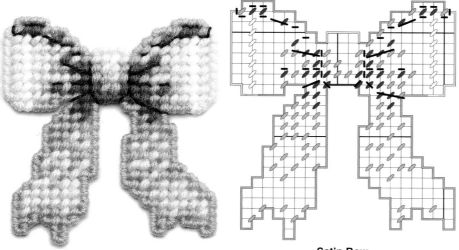

COLOR KEY
Satin Bow

Yards	Worsted Weight Yarn
1 (1m)	□ White #1
3 (2.8m)	▩ Pale rose #755
1 (1m)	■ Cameo rose #759
2 (1.9m)	Uncoded areas are lily pink #719 Continental Stitches
	∕ Lily pink #719 Overcasting

#5 Pearl Cotton

1 (1m)	∕ Ultra dark coffee brown #938 Backstitch and Straight Stitch

Color numbers given are for Coats & Clark Red Heart Classic worsted weight yarn Art. E267 and DMC #5 pearl cotton.

Satin Bow
21 holes x 23 holes
Cut 1

■ **Girls, Girls, Girls** ■

Wishes Fairy

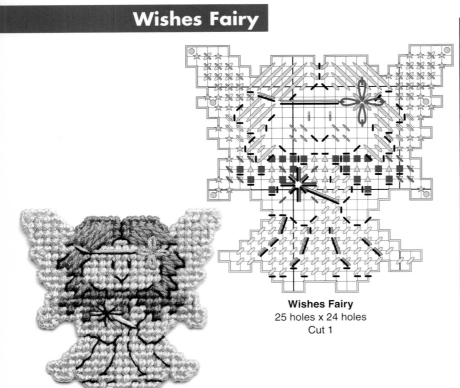

Wishes Fairy
25 holes x 24 holes
Cut 1

COLOR KEY
Wishes Fairy

Yards		Plastic Canvas Yarn
3 (2.8m)	⊘	Pink #07
1 (1m)	◇	Lemon #20
2 (1.9m)	△	Fern #23
1 (1m)	■	Christmas green #28
1 (1m)	▽	Baby blue #36
3 (2.8m)	☆	Silver #37
2 (1.9m)	⊘	Camel #43
		Uncoded background is pale peach #56 Continental Stitches
	⁄	Pale peach #56 Overcasting
	⁄	Silver #37 Straight Stitch

Heavy (#32) Braid

1 (1m)	⊘	Chartreuse #015 (2 strands)
1 (1m)	⁄	Star yellow #091 Straight Stitch
	⁄	Star pink #092 Straight Stitch
2 (1.9m)	⁄	Periwinkle #9294 Straight Stitch
	⚘	Periwinkle #9294 Lazy Daisy Stitch
	○	Star yellow #091 French Knot (1 wrap)

#5 Pearl Cotton

3 (2.8m)	⁄	Black (1 strand) Backstitch and Straight Stitch
	⁄	Black (4 strands) Straight Stitch (eyes)

Color numbers given are for Uniek Needloft plastic canvas yarn and Kreinik Heavy (#32) Braid.

Dreams Fairy

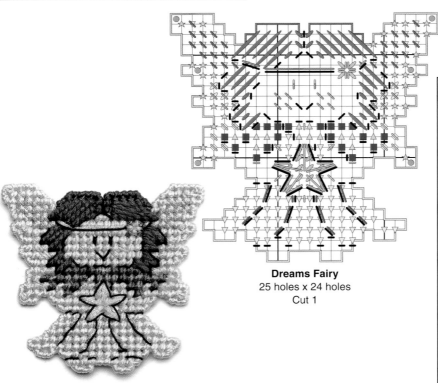

Dreams Fairy
25 holes x 24 holes
Cut 1

COLOR KEY
Dreams Fairy

Yards		Plastic Canvas Yarn
1 (1m)	⊘	Pink #07
2 (1.9m)	⬮	Cinnamon #15
1 (1m)	◇	Lemon #20
1 (1m)	△	Fern #23
1 (1m)	■	Christmas green #28
3 (2.8m)	▽	Baby blue #36
2 (1.9m)	☆	Silver #37
2 (1.9m)		Uncoded background is pale peach #56 Continental Stitches
	⁄	Pale peach #56 Overcasting
	⁄	Silver #37 Straight Stitch

Heavy (#32) Braid

1 (1m)	⊘	Chartreuse #015 (2 strands)
2 (1.9m)	⊘	Star yellow #091 (2 strands)
	⁄	Star yellow #091 Straight Stitch
1 (1m)	⁄	Star pink #092 Straight Stitch
1 (1m)	⁄	Periwinkle #9294 Straight Stitch
	○	Star pink #092 French Knot (1 wrap)

#5 Pearl Cotton

3 (2.8m)	⁄	Black (1 strand) Backstitch and Straight Stitch
	⁄	Black (4 strands) Straight Stitch (eyes)

Color numbers given are for Uniek Needloft plastic canvas yarn and Kreinik Heavy (#32) Braid.

Affection Fairy

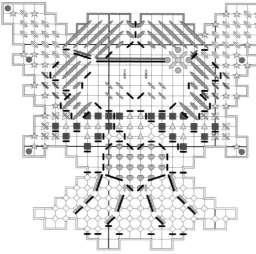

Affection Fairy
25 holes x 24 holes
Cut 1

COLOR KEY
Affection Fairy

Yards	Plastic Canvas Yarn
1 (1m)	⬚ Pink #07
2 (1.9m)	⬚ Maple #13
3 (2.8m)	◇ Lemon #20
1 (1m)	△ Fern #23
1 (1m)	■ Christmas green #28
1 (1m)	▽ Baby blue #36
2 (1.9m)	☆ Silver #37
2 (1.9m)	Uncoded background is pale peach #56 Continental Stitches
	⬚ Pale peach #56 Overcasting
	⬚ Silver #37 Straight Stitch

Heavy (#32) Braid

1 (1m)	⬚ Chartreuse #015 (2 strands)
2 (1.9m)	♥ Star pink #092 (2 strands)
1 (1m)	⬚ Star yellow #091 Straight Stitch
1 (1m)	⬚ Star pink #092 Straight Stitch
1 (1m)	⬚ Periwinkle #9294 Straight Stitch
	● Star yellow #09 French Knot (2 wraps)
	● Star pink #092 French Knot (2 wraps)
	● Periwinkle #9294 French Knot (1 wrap)

#5 Pearl Cotton

3 (2.8m)	⬚ Black (1 strand) Backstitch and Straight Stitch
	⬚ Black (4 strands) Straight Stitch (eyes)

Color numbers given are for Uniek Needloft plastic canvas yarn and Kreinik Heavy (#32) Braid.

Fairy Godmother

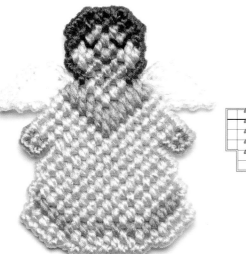

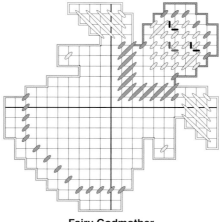

Fairy Godmother
20 holes x 20 holes
Cut 1

COLOR KEY
Fairy Godmother

Yards	Plastic Canvas Yarn
1 (1m)	☐ Pink #07
1 (1m)	■ Brown #15
1 (1m)	■ Sail blue #35
1 (1m)	☐ Pale peach #56
1 (1m)	☐ White #41
3 (2.8m)	Uncoded areas are baby blue #36 Continental Stitches
	⬚ Baby blue #36 Overcasting

#5 Pearl Cotton

1 (1m)	⬚ Black Backstitch
1 (1m)	⬚ Red Backstitch

Color numbers given are for Uniek Needloft plastic canvas yarn.

Jeweled Tiara

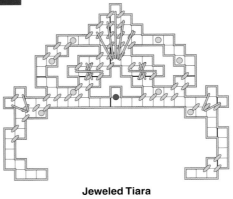

Jeweled Tiara
21 holes x 17 holes
Cut 1

Ribbon-Trimmed Heart Frame

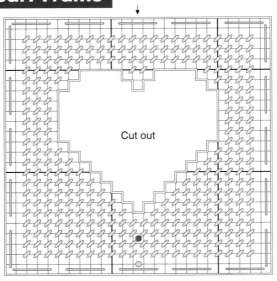

Cut out

Ribbon-Trimmed Heart Frame
25 holes x 25 holes
Cut 1

Baby-Blue Bow Heart

Continue pattern

Baby-Blue Bow Heart
25 holes x 21 holes
Cut 1

Glove Heart

Illustration on page 167

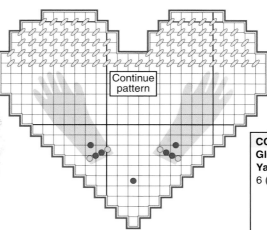

Continue pattern

Glove Heart
25 holes x 21 holes
Cut 1

COLOR KEY
Glove Heart

Yards	Plastic Canvas Yarn
6 (5.5m)	☐ Pink #07
	— Attach ½-inch/1.3cm-wide white lace trim
	▨ Attach glove (see pattern)
	● Attach ½-inch/1.3cm-wide pink ribbon rose with leaves
	○ Attach 4mm gold bead
	● Attach 3mm gold bead

Color number given is for Uniek Needloft plastic canvas yarn.

Baby-Blue Heart

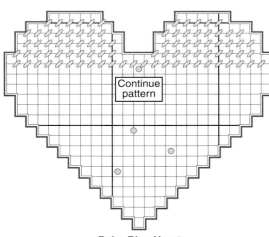

Continue pattern

Baby-Blue Heart
25 holes x 21 holes
Cut 1

COLOR KEY
Baby-Blue Heart

Yards	Plastic Canvas Yarn
6 (5.5m)	☐ Baby blue #36
1 (1m)	∕ White #41 Overcasting
	— Attach ½-inch/1.3cm-wide white lace trim
	○ Attach 2-inch/5cm-wide pink layered die-cut bow or bow of choice
	○ Attach die-cut layered daisies or flowers desired

Color numbers given are for Uniek Needloft plastic canvas yarn.

Lollipop

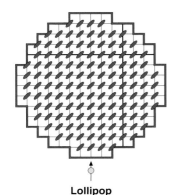

Lollipop
14 holes x 14 holes
Cut 1

COLOR KEY
Lollipop

Yards	Plastic Canvas Yarn
2 (1.9m)	■ Christmas red #02
	↟ Attach 5-inch/12.7cm lollipop stick
	○ Wrap lollipop with clear plastic then tie a yellow satin ribbon bow around plastic and lollipop stick

Color number given is for Uniek Needloft plastic canvas yarn.

Feminine Finery Red Hat

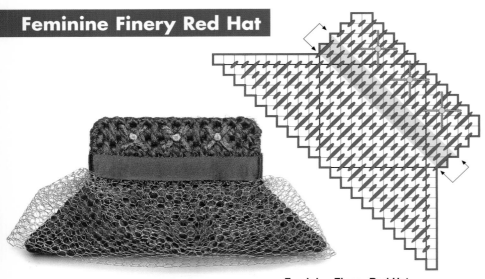

Feminine Finery Red Hat
25 holes x 25 holes
Cut 1

COLOR KEY
Feminine Finery Red Hat

Yards	Plastic Canvas Yarn
5 (4.6m)	■ Red #01
1 (1m)	⁄ Bright purple #64 Straight Stitch
1 (1m)	○ Yellow #57 (1-ply) French Knot
	▨ Attach raw edge purple netting (4½ x 7 inches/11.4 x 17.8cm folded in half lengthwise and gathered along raw edge)

³⁄₈-Inch/1cm-Wide Satin Ribbon
↪ Glue 5³⁄₈-inch/13.7cm length purple over raw edges of netting

Color numbers given are for Uniek Needloft plastic canvas yarn.

Feminine Finery Purse

 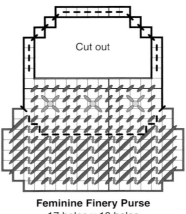

Feminine Finery Purse
17 holes x 18 holes
Cut 1

COLOR KEY
Feminine Finery Purse

Yards	Plastic Canvas Yarn
3 (2.8m)	■ Red #01
1 (1m)	▨ Bright purple #64
1 (1m)	⁄ Black #00 Backstitch and Overcasting
	⁄ Red #01 Backstitch
1 (1m)	⁄ Bright purple #64 Backstitch
	○ Yellow #57 (1-ply) French Knot

Color numbers given are for Uniek Needloft plastic canvas yarn.

Feminine Finery Hanger

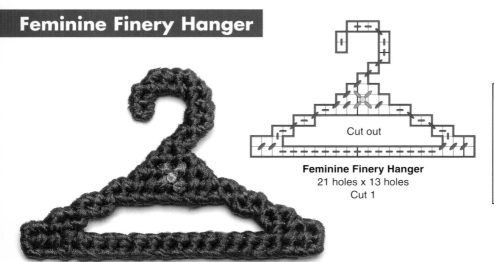

Feminine Finery Hanger
21 holes x 13 holes
Cut 1

COLOR KEY
Feminine Finery Hanger

Yards	Plastic Canvas Yarn
3 (2.8m)	■ Red #01
1 (1m)	▨ Bright purple #64
	⁄ Red #01 Backstitch
1 (1m)	○ Yellow #57 (1-ply) French Knot

Color numbers given are for Uniek Needloft plastic canvas yarn.

Feminine Finery Red Shoe

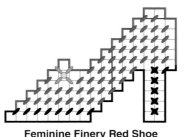

Feminine Finery Red Shoe
16 holes x 11 holes
Cut 1

COLOR KEY
Feminine Finery Red Shoe

Yards	Plastic Canvas Yarn
1 (1m)	■ Black #00
3 (2.8m)	■ Red #01
1 (1m)	▨ Bright purple #64
1 (1m)	○ Yellow #57 (1-ply) French Knot

Color numbers given are for Uniek Needloft plastic canvas yarn.

Maiden With Bouquet

Maiden With Bouquet
25 holes x 25 holes
Cut 1

COLOR KEY
Maiden With Bouquet

Yards	Plastic Canvas Yarn
1 (1m)	■ Black #00
1 (1m)	▢ Pink #07
2 (1.9m)	▨ Tangerine #11
2 (1.9m)	▢ White #41
1 (1m)	▢ Pale peach #56
3 (2.8m)	Uncoded areas are sail blue #35 Continental Stitches
	⁄ Sail blue #35 Overcasting
1 (1m)	⁄ Holly #27 Straight Stitch
2 (1.9m)	⁄ Royal #32 Backstitch and Straight Stitch
	⤸ Royal #32 Lazy Daisy Stitch
	● Black #00 French Knot
1 (1m)	● Christmas red #02 French Knot
1 (1m)	○ Yellow #57 French Knot

Color numbers given are for Uniek Needloft plastic canvas yarn.

Cheerleader

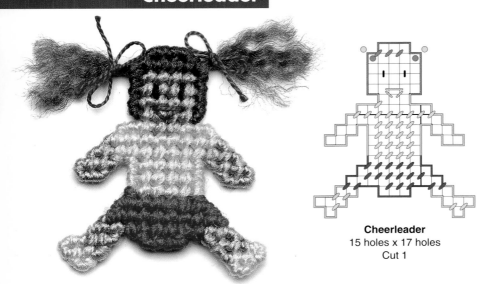

Cheerleader
15 holes x 17 holes
Cut 1

Black Ankle Strap Shoe

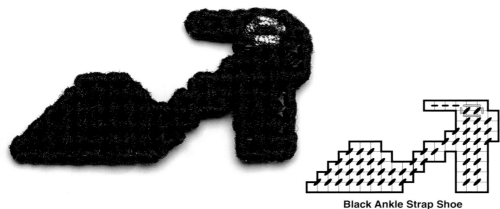

Black Ankle Strap Shoe
18 holes x 9 holes
Cut 1

Flowered Spike Heel

Flowered Spike Heel
16 holes x 10 holes
Cut 1

ink Polka-Dot Sling Back

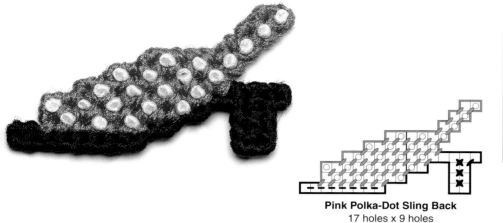

Pink Polka-Dot Sling Back
17 holes x 9 holes
Cut 1

Glass Slipper

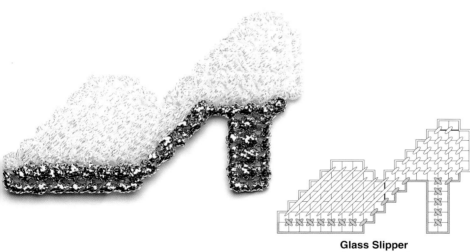

Glass Slipper
18 holes x 11 holes
Cut 1

Casual Checked Mule

Casual Checked Mule
18 holes x 5 holes
Cut 1

Red Bow

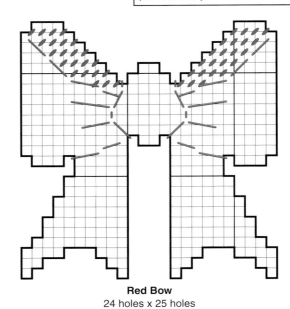

Red Bow
24 holes x 25 holes
Cut 1

Large Red Hat

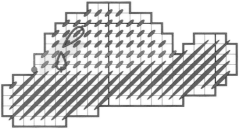

Large Red Hat
22 holes x 12 holes
Cut 1

Small Red Hat

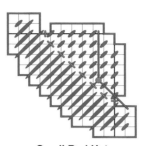

COLOR KEY
Small Red Hat

Yards	Worsted Weight Yarn
3 (2.8m)	■ Cherry red #912
1 (1m)	╱ Amethyst #588 Backstitch
	╱ Glue ¹/₈-inch/0.3cm-wide green satin ribbon
	● Attach small purple flower

Color numbers given are for Coats & Clark Red Heart Classic worsted weight yarn Art. E267.

Small Red Hat
12 holes x 12 holes
Cut 1

Hat, Purse & Shoe Show

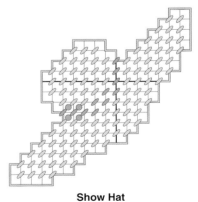

COLOR KEY
Hat, Purse & Shoe Show

Yards	Plastic Canvas Yarn
5 (4.6m)	☐ Fern #23
2 (1.9m)	▨ Watermelon #55
	╱ Watermelon #55 Straight Stitch
	● Watermelon #55 (³/₈-inch/ 1cm-high) loop

Color numbers given are for Uniek Needloft plastic canvas yarn.

Cut out

Show Purse
12 holes x 14 holes
Cut 1

Show Shoe
17 holes x 7 holes
Cut 1

Show Hat
17 holes x 17 holes
Cut 1

Holidays

Fast and easy projects for year-round holidays make great last-minute gifts!

Happy New Year Banner

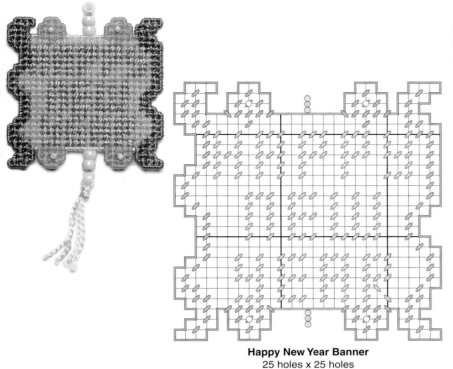

Happy New Year Banner
25 holes x 25 holes
Cut 1

COLOR KEY
Happy New Year Banner

Yards	Plastic Canvas Yarn
3 (2.8m)	☐ Fern #23
3 (2.8m)	☐ Bright blue #60
2 (1.9m)	☐ Bright pink #62
4 (3.7m)	Uncoded background is bright orange #58 Continental Stitches
2 (1.9m)	✏ Yellow #57 Overcasting
	○ Attach yellow E bead
	○ Attach 6 x 9mm yellow pony bead on yellow #57 for hanger
	○ Attach 6 x 9mm blue pony bead on yellow #57 for hanger
	○ Attach 6 x 9mm yellow pony bead on 3-inch/7.6cm-long yellow #57 tail
	○ Attach 6 x 9mm blue pony bead on 3-inch/7.6cm-long yellow #57 tail

Color numbers given are for Uniek Needloft plastic canvas yarn.

Happy New Year Ball

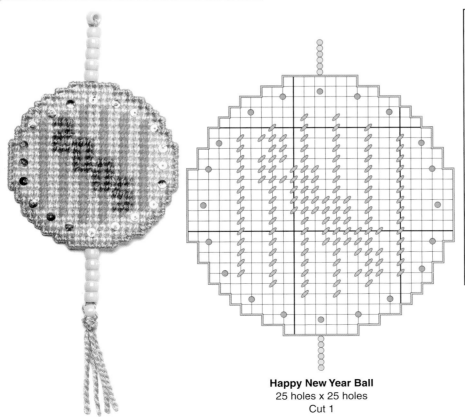

Happy New Year Ball
25 holes x 25 holes
Cut 1

COLOR KEY
Happy New Year Ball

Yards	Plastic Canvas Yarn
1 (1m)	☐ Fern #23
2 (1.9m)	☐ Bright pink #62
6 (5.5m)	Uncoded background is yellow #57 Continental Stitches
2 (1.9m)	✏ Bright blue #60 Overcasting
	● Attach 5mm orange sequin
	○ Attach 6 x 9mm yellow pony bead on bright blue #60 for hanger
	○ Attach 6 x 9mm blue pony bead on bright blue #60 for hanger
	○ Attach 6 x 9mm yellow pony bead on 4-inch/10.2cm-long bright blue #60 tail
	○ Attach 6 x 9mm blue pony bead on 4-inch/10.2cm-long bright blue #60 tail

Color numbers given are for Uniek Needloft plastic canvas yarn.

Happy New Year Hat & Mask

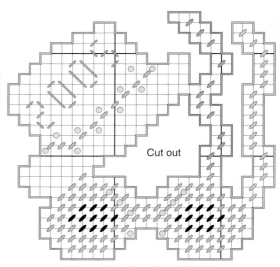

COLOR KEY

Happy New Year Hat & Mask

Yards	Plastic Canvas Yarn
1 (1m)	■ Black #00
1 (1m)	▨ Bright orange #58
1 (1m)	▨ Bright blue #60
3 (2.8m)	▨ Bright pink #62
3 (2.8m)	Uncoded areas are fern #23 Continental Stitches
	⁄ Fern #23 Overcasting
	⁄ Bright pink #62 Backstitch
	○ Attach yellow E bead

Color numbers given are for Uniek Needloft plastic canvas yarn.

Cut out

Happy New Year Hat & Mask
25 holes x 24 holes
Cut 1

Happy New Year Horn & Notes

COLOR KEY

Happy New Year Horn & Notes

Yards	Plastic Canvas Yarn
1 (1m)	▨ Fern #23
2 (1.9m)	▢ Yellow #57
2 (1.9m)	▨ Bright orange #58
2 (1.9m)	▢ Bright blue #60
2 (1.9m)	▨ Bright pink #62
	⁄ Fern #23 Backstitch
	⁄ Bright pink #62 Backstitch
	○ Attach yellow E bead

Color numbers given are for Uniek Needloft plastic canvas yarn.

Happy New Year Horn & Notes
25 holes x 25 holes
Cut 1

Figure Skate

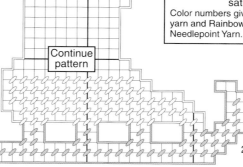

Continue pattern

COLOR KEY

Figure Skate

Yards	Plastic Canvas Yarn
4 (3.7m)	▢ White #41
	⅛-Inch/0.3cm Metallic Needlepoint Yarn
2 (1.9m)	▨ Silver #PC2
	— Attach ³⁄₈-inch/1cm-wide red satin ribbon bow

Color numbers given are for Uniek Needloft plastic canvas yarn and Rainbow Gallery Plastic Canvas 7 Metallic Needlepoint Yarn.

Figure Skate
25 holes x 25 holes
Cut 1

Blue Mitten

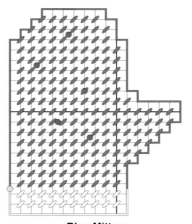

Blue Mitten
16 holes x 20 holes
Cut 1

COLOR KEY
Blue Mitten

Yards	Plastic Canvas Yarn
3 (2.8m)	■ Royal #32
	Worsted Weight Yarn
1 (1m)	☐ Winter frost #501
	● Attach white snowflake button
	○ Attach two ½-inch/1.3cm white pompoms on ends of winter frost #501 tie

Color numbers given are for Uniek Needloft plastic canvas yarn and Lion Brand Wool-Ease worsted weight yarn Article #620.

Pint-Size Evergreen

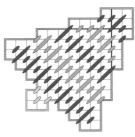

Pint-Size Evergreen
12 holes x 12 holes
Cut 1

COLOR KEY
Pint-Size Evergreen

Yards	Plastic Canvas Yarn
1 (1m)	☐ Maple #13
2 (1.9m)	▨ Christmas green #28
1 (1m)	■ Forest #29

Color numbers given are for Uniek Needloft plastic canvas yarn.

Blushing Snowman

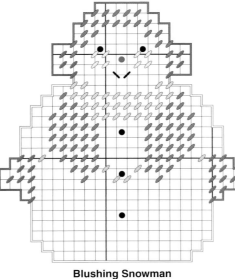

Blushing Snowman
23 holes x 25 holes
Cut 1

COLOR KEY
Blushing Snowman

Yards	Plastic Canvas Yarn
1 (1m)	■ Christmas red #02
1 (1m)	☐ Pink #07
2 (1.9m)	■ Holly #27
1 (1m)	☐ Sail blue #35
1 (1m)	☐ Gray #38
4 (3.7m)	Uncoded areas are white #41 Continental Stitches
	⁄ White #41 Overcasting
1 (1m)	✓ Black #00 Backstitch
	● Black #00 French Knot
	● Christmas red #02 French Knot

Color numbers given are for Uniek Needloft plastic canvas yarn.

Jolly Snowman

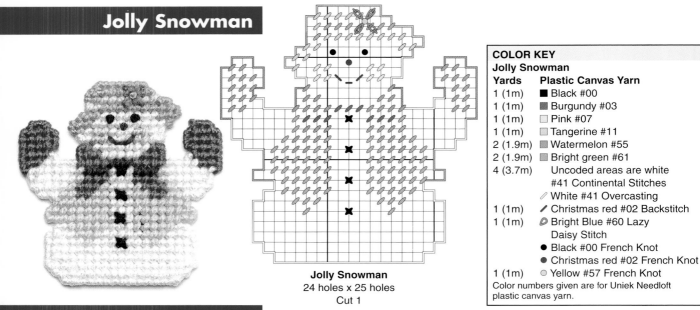

Jolly Snowman
24 holes x 25 holes
Cut 1

Pint-Size Snowman

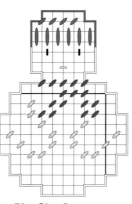

Pint-Size Snowman
12 holes x 18 holes
Cut 1

Snowman

Illustrations on page 168

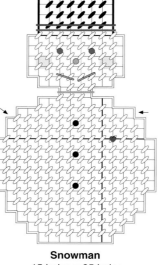

Snowman
15 holes x 25 holes
Cut 1

Snowman With Blue Scarf

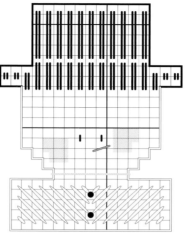

Snowman With Blue Scarf
17 holes x 22 holes
Cut 1

COLOR KEY
Snowman With Blue Scarf

Yards	Plastic Canvas Yarn
4 (3.7m)	☐ White #41
	Uncoded areas are white #41 Continental Stitches
3 (2.8m)	✏ Black #00 Straight Stitch
1 (1m)	✏ Bittersweet #52 (2-strand) Straight Stitch
	● Black #00 French Knot
	— Tie ¼-inch/0.6cm-wide light blue satin ribbon around snowman
	▦ Brush yarn in this area with light pink blush

Color numbers given are for Uniek Needloft plastic canvas yarn.

Lovely Snowman

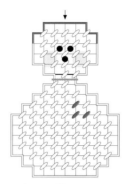

Lovey Snowman
10 holes x 15 holes
Cut 1

COLOR KEY
Lovey Snowman

Yards	Plastic Canvas Yarn
1 (1m)	▦ Christmas red #02
3 (2.8m)	☐ White #41
1 (1m)	● Black #00 (1-ply) French Knot
1 (1m)	◉ Bittersweet #52 (1-ply) French Knot
	— Tie ⅛-inch/0.3cm-wide red satin ribbon around snowman
	↓ Attach ⅜-inch/1cm red pompom
	▦ Brush yarn in this area with pink blush

Color numbers given are for Uniek Needloft plastic canvas yarn.

Let It Snow Snowman

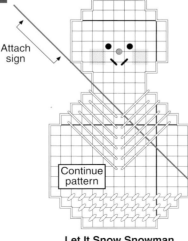

Attach sign

Continue pattern

Let It Snow Snowman
13 holes x 22 holes
Cut 1

COLOR KEY
Let It Snow Snowman

Yards	Plastic Canvas Yarn
6 (5.5m)	▦ White #41
1 (1m)	Black #00 (1-ply) Backstitch
	✏ White #41 (1-ply) Straight Stitch
	● Black #00 (1-ply) French Knot
1 (1m)	◉ Bittersweet #52 (1-ply) French Knot
	↘ Slip and glue 3½-inch/8.9cm natural craft pick under arm
	↗ Attach "Let It Snow!" sign (1¼ x ¾-inch/3.2 x 1.9cm piece from brown paper bag)
	▦ Brush yarn in this area with pink blush

Color numbers given are for Uniek Needloft plastic canvas yarn.

Valentine Kiss

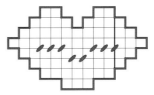

Valentine Kiss
13 holes x 8 holes
Cut 1

COLOR KEY
Valentine Kiss

Yards	Plastic Canvas Yarn
1 (1m)	■ Red #01
2 (1.9m)	Uncoded background is watermelon #55 Continental Stitches

Color numbers given are for Uniek Needloft plastic canvas yarn.

Red Flower Heart

Illustration on page 168

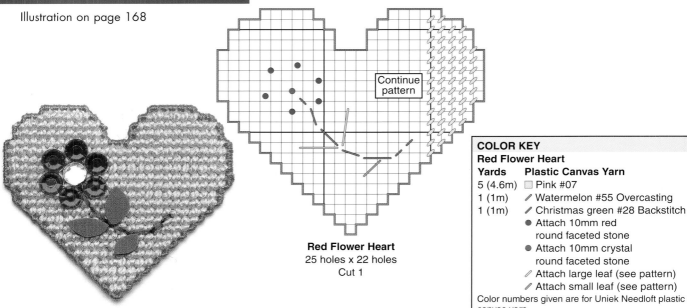

Continue pattern

Red Flower Heart
25 holes x 22 holes
Cut 1

COLOR KEY
Red Flower Heart

Yards	Plastic Canvas Yarn
5 (4.6m)	☐ Pink #07
1 (1m)	⁄ Watermelon #55 Overcasting
1 (1m)	⁄ Christmas green #28 Backstitch
	● Attach 10mm red round faceted stone
	● Attach 10mm crystal round faceted stone
	⁄ Attach large leaf (see pattern)
	⁄ Attach small leaf (see pattern)

Color numbers given are for Uniek Needloft plastic canvas yarn.

Mirror Heart

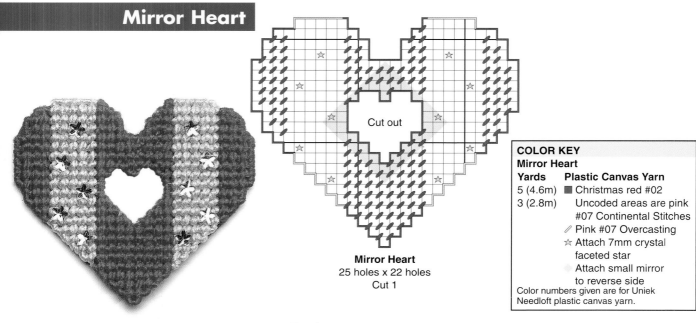

Cut out

Mirror Heart
25 holes x 22 holes
Cut 1

COLOR KEY
Mirror Heart

Yards	Plastic Canvas Yarn
5 (4.6m)	■ Christmas red #02
3 (2.8m)	Uncoded areas are pink #07 Continental Stitches
	⁄ Pink #07 Overcasting
	☆ Attach 7mm crystal faceted star
	Attach small mirror to reverse side

Color numbers given are for Uniek Needloft plastic canvas yarn.

Striped Heart

Striped Heart
25 holes x 22 holes
Cut 1

Irishman

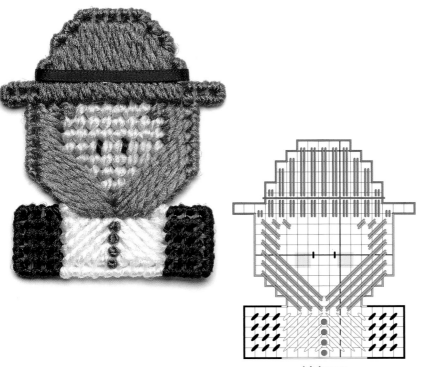

Irishman
17 holes x 21 holes
Cut 1

Spring Egg 1

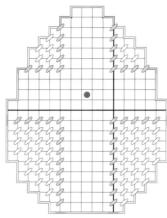

Spring Egg 1
15 holes x 20 holes
Cut 1

Spring Egg 2

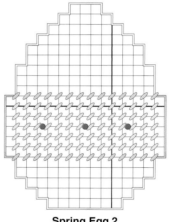

Spring Egg 2
15 holes x 20 holes
Cut 1

Spring Egg 3

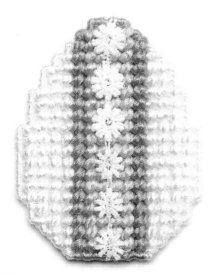

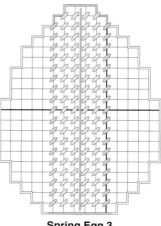

Spring Egg 3
15 holes x 20 holes
Cut 1

Spring Egg 4

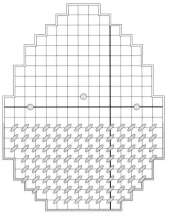

Spring Egg 4
15 holes x 20 holes
Cut 1

COLOR KEY
Spring Egg 4

Yards	Plastic Canvas Yarn
1 (1m)	☐ Moss #25
2 (1.9m)	☐ Lilac #45
3 (3.7m)	Uncoded areas are white #41 Continental Stitches
	∕ White #41 Overcasting
	○ Attach yellow flower appliqué

Color numbers given are for Uniek Needloft plastic canvas yarn.

Peek-a-Boo Bunny

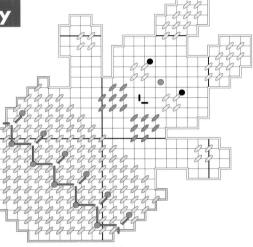

Peek-a-Boo Bunny
24 holes x 24 holes
Cut 1

COLOR KEY
Peek-a-Boo Bunny

Yards	Plastic Canvas Yarn
1 (1m)	☐ Pink #07
1 (1m)	☐ Fern #23
1 (1m)	☐ Sail blue #35
2 (1.9m)	☐ Yellow #57
1 (1m)	☐ Bright purple #64
3 (2.8m)	Uncoded areas are white #41 Continental Stitches
	∕ White #41 Overcasting
1 (1m)	∕ Black #00 (1-ply) Backstitch
	∕ Christmas green #28 (1-ply) Backstitch
	● Black #00 (1-ply) French Knot
	● Watermelon #55 (1-ply) French Knot
	● Bright purple #64 (2-ply) French Knot

Color numbers given are for Uniek Needloft plastic canvas yarn.

Golden Cross

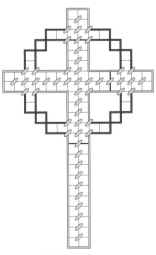

Golden Cross
14 holes x 23 holes
Cut 1

COLOR KEY
Golden Cross

Yards	Solid Metallic Craft Cord
2 (1.9m)	☐ Solid gold #55020
	Plastic Canvas Yarn
1 (1m)	∕ Burgundy #03 Overcasting

Color numbers given are for Uniek Needloft solid metallic craft cord and plastic canvas yarn.

Pastel Easter Egg

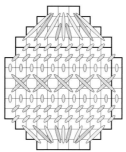

Pastel Easter Egg
11 holes x 14 holes
Cut 1 from pastel
plastic canvas of choice

Bunny With Egg

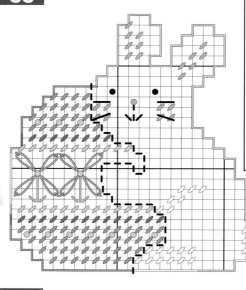

Bunny With Egg
25 holes x 25 holes
Cut 1

Decorated Egg

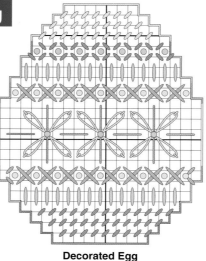

Decorated Egg
19 holes x 23 holes
Cut 1

Pink Easter Egg

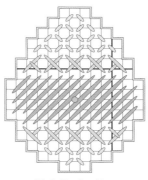

Pink Easter Egg
13 holes x 16 holes
Cut 1

COLOR KEY
Pink Easter Egg

Yards	Plastic Canvas Yarn
3 (2.8m)	☐ Pink #07
1 (1m)	☐ Moss #25
1 (1m)	☐ Lilac #45
	○ Attach ¾-inch/1.9cm gold butterfly charm

Color numbers given are for Uniek Needloft plastic canvas yarn.

Blue Easter Egg

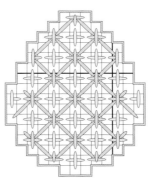

Blue Easter Egg
13 holes x 16 holes
Cut 1

COLOR KEY
Blue Easter Egg

Yards	Plastic Canvas Yarn
2 (1.9m)	☐ Pink #07
2 (1.9m)	☐ Lemon #20
1 (1m)	☐ Sail blue #35

Color numbers given are for Uniek Needloft plastic canvas yarn.

Dressed-Up Bunny

Dressed-Up Bunny
25 holes x 25 holes
Cut 1

COLOR KEY
Dressed-Up Bunny

Yards	Plastic Canvas Yarn
1 (1m)	☐ Pink #07
2 (1.9m)	☐ Pumpkin #12
2 (1.9m)	☐ Moss #25
2 (1.9m)	☐ Christmas green #28
1 (1m)	☐ Royal #32
1 (1m)	☐ Sail blue #35
2 (1.9m)	☐ Lilac #45
1 (1m)	☐ Purple #46
3 (2.8m)	Uncoded areas are white #41 Continental Stitch
	⁄ White #41 Overcasting
1 (1m)	╱ Black #00 Backstitch
	● Black #00 French Knot
1 (1m)	● Watermelon #55 French Knot

Color numbers given are for Uniek Needloft plastic canvas yarn.

Egg 1
15 holes x 20 holes
Cut 1

COLOR KEY
Egg 1

Yards	Plastic Canvas Yarn
1 (1m)	☐ Tangerine #11
1 (1m)	☐ Fern #23
1 (1m)	☐ Yellow #57
2 (1.9m)	Uncoded areas are bright purple #64 Continental Stitches
✎	Bright purple #64 Overcasting

Color numbers given are for Uniek Needloft plastic canvas yarn.

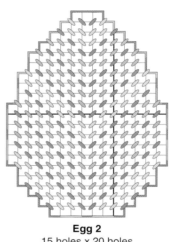

Egg 2
15 holes x 20 holes
Cut 1

COLOR KEY
Egg 2

Yards	Plastic Canvas Yarn
1 (1m)	☐ Tangerine #11
1 (1m)	☐ Fern #23
1 (1m)	☐ Yellow #57
2 (1.9m)	■ Bright purple #64

Color numbers given are for Uniek Needloft plastic canvas yarn.

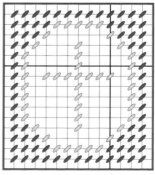

Framed Cross
14 holes x 16 holes
Cut 1

COLOR KEY
Framed Cross

Yards	Plastic Canvas Yarn
3 (2.8m)	■ Burgundy #03
2 (1.9m)	Uncoded area is white #41 Continental Stitches
	Metallic Craft Cord
1 (1m)	☐ Gold #55001

Color numbers given are for Uniek Needloft plastic canvas yarn and metallic craft cord.

Egg 3

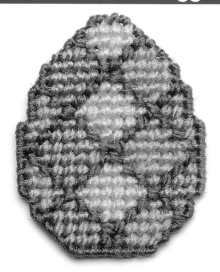

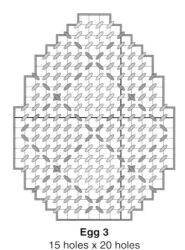

Egg 3
15 holes x 20 holes
Cut 1

COLOR KEY
Egg 3

Yards	Plastic Canvas Yarn
2 (1.9m)	☐ Tangerine #11
2 (1.9m)	☐ Fern #23
1 (1m)	☐ Yellow #57
2 (1.9m)	■ Bright purple #64

Color numbers given are for Uniek
Needloft plastic canvas yarn.

Egg 4

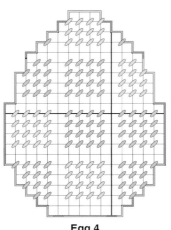

Egg 4
15 holes x 20 holes
Cut 1

COLOR KEY
Egg 4

Yards	Plastic Canvas Yarn
1 (1m)	☐ Tangerine #11
1 (1m)	☐ Fern #23
2 (1.9m)	☐ Yellow #57
2 (1.9m)	Uncoded areas are bright purple #64 Continental Stitches
	╱ Bright purple #64 Overcasting

Color numbers given are for Uniek Needloft
plastic canvas yarn.

Purple & Pearl Cross

Purple & Pearl Cross
13 holes x 25 holes
Cut 1

COLOR KEY
Purple & Pearl Cross

Yards	Plastic Canvas Yarn
1 (1m)	■ Bright purple #64
	1/16-Inch/0.2cm Metallic Needlepoint Yarn
3 (2.8m)	╱ White pearl #PM70 Overcasting and Straight Stitch
	○ White pearl #PM70 Lark's Head Knot

Color numbers given are for Uniek Needloft plastic canvas
yarn and Rainbow Gallery Plastic Canvas 10 Metallic
Needlepoint Yarn.

Green & Gold Cross

Green & Gold Cross
13 holes x 25 holes
Cut 1

Pink & Gold Cross

Pink & Gold Cross
17 holes x 25 holes
Cut 1

Blue & Silver Cross

Blue & Silver Cross
17 holes x 25 holes
Cut 1

Mortarboard

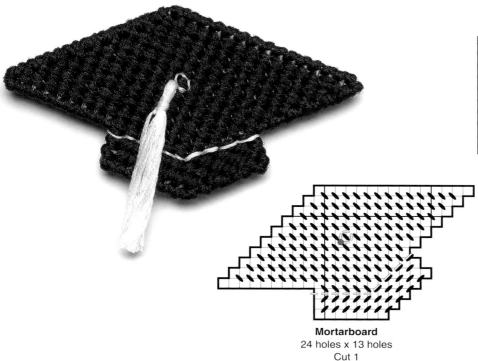

Mortarboard
24 holes x 13 holes
Cut 1

Uncle Sam

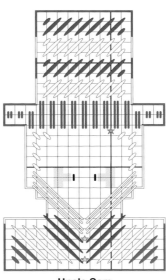

Uncle Sam
15 holes x 25 holes
Cut 1

Striped Firecracker

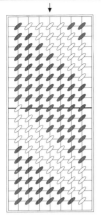

Striped Firecracker
8 holes x 19 holes
Cut 1

Three-Star Firecracker

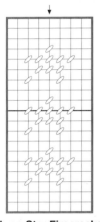

Three-Star Firecracker
8 holes x 19 holes
Cut 1

One-Star Firecracker

One-Star Firecracker
8 holes x 19 holes
Cut 1

Patriotic Heart

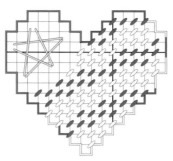

Patriotic Heart
15 holes x 14 holes
Cut 1

COLOR KEY
Patriotic Heart

Yards	Plastic Canvas Yarn
2 (1.9m)	■ Christmas red #02
2 (1.9m)	□ White #41
1 (1m)	Uncoded areas are royal #32 Continental Stitches
	╱ Royal #32 Overcasting
	6-Strand Embroidery Floss
1 (1m)	╱ White Straight Stitch

Color numbers given are for Uniek Needloft plastic canvas yarn.

Patriotic Star

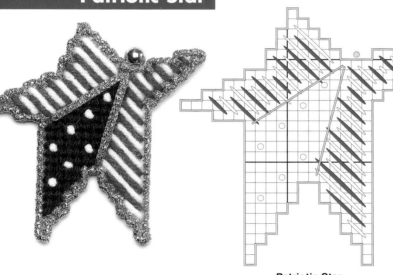

Patriotic Star
24 holes x 25 holes
Cut 1

COLOR KEY
Patriotic Star

Yards	Worsted Weight Yarn
6 (5.5m)	□ White #1
2 (1.9m)	■ Cherry red #912
4 (3.7m)	Uncoded areas are soft navy #853 Continental Stitches
	○ White #1 French Knot
	¹⁄₈-Inch/0.3cm Metallic Needlepoint Yarn
3 (2.8m)	╱ Gold #PC1 Straight Stitch and Overcasting
	● Attach 10mm gold bead

Color numbers given are for Coats & Clark Red Heart Classic worsted weight yarn Art. E267 and Rainbow Gallery Plastic Canvas 7 Metallic Needlepoint Yarn.

Heart & Stripes Forever

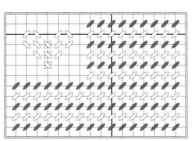

Heart & Stripes Forever
17 holes x 12 holes
Cut 1

COLOR KEY
Heart & Stripes Forever

Yards	Plastic Canvas Yarn
2 (1.9m)	■ Christmas red #02
2 (1.9m)	□ White #41
1 (1m)	Uncoded area is royal #32 Continental Stitches
1 (1m)	╱ Gold #17 Overcasting

Color numbers given are for Uniek Needloft plastic canvas yarn.

Jester's Hat

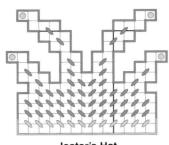

Jester's Hat
15 holes x 12 holes
Cut 1

COLOR KEY
Jester's Hat

Yards	Heavy (#32) Braid
1 (1m)	☐ Gold #002
1 (1m)	■ Purple #012
1 (1m)	■ Tropical teal #339
	○ Attach 6mm gold jingle bell

Color numbers given are for Kreinik Heavy (#32) Braid.

Masquerade Half-Mask

COLOR KEY
Masquerade Half-Mask

Yards	Heavy (#32) Braid
3 (2.8m)	■ Tropical teal #339
1 (1m)	⁄ Gold #002 Overcasting
	○ Attach 6mm gold oval bead
	○ Attach 5mm gold round bead
	❨ Attach feather

Color numbers given are for Kreinik Heavy (#32) Braid.

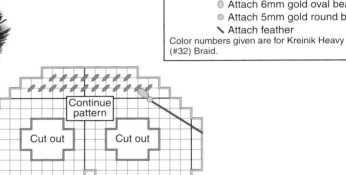

Continue pattern

Cut out   Cut out

Masquerade Half-Mask
21 holes x 13 holes
Cut 1

Masquerade Mask

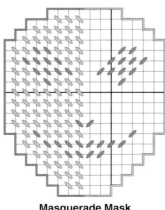

Masquerade Mask
15 holes x 18 holes
Cut 1

COLOR KEY
Masquerade Mask

Yards	Heavy (#32) Braid
2 (1.9m)	☐ Gold #002
1 (1m)	■ Tropical teal #339
2 (1.9m)	Uncoded areas are purple #012 Continental Stitches

Color numbers given are for Kreinik Heavy (#32) Braid.

Witch

Witch Bow Tie
Cut 1 from
black craft foam

COLOR KEY
Witch

Yards	Plastic Canvas Yarn
1 (1m)	■ Black #00
1 (1m)	▦ Pumpkin #12
2 (1.9m)	▦ Fern #23
1 (1m)	☐ Pale peach #56
4 (3.7m)	Uncoded areas are bright purple #64 Continental Stitches
	╱ Bright purple #64 Overcasting
	⌐ Pumpkin #12 Turkey Loop Stitch (³/₈-inch/1cm-long, cut and frayed)
1 (1m)	**6-Strand Embroidery Floss**
	╱ Black Backstitch
	● Black French Knot
	● Attach 3mm orange bead
	● Attach bow tie (see pattern)
	− Attach hat brim (see pattern)
	◣ Attach hat crown (1¹/₁₆ x 1¹/₂-inch/ 2.7 x 3.8cm black craft foam triangle)
	⇄ Attach ghost button
	○ Attach nose (³/₈-inch/1cm-long pale peach polymer clay) (see general instructions)

Color numbers given are for Uniek Needloft plastic canvas yarn.

Witch
22 holes x 25 holes
Cut 1

Witch Hat Brim
Cut 1 from
black craft foam
Slip over head

Ghostly Night

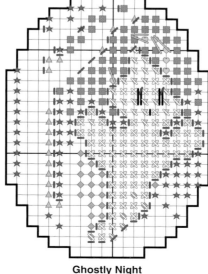

Ghostly Night
19 holes x 25 holes
Cut 1

COLOR KEY
Ghostly Night

Yards	Worsted Weight Yarn
1 (1m)	⊘ Maize #261
1 (1m)	△ Warm brown #336
1 (1m)	◆ Nickel #401
1 (1m)	⊘ Silver #412
1 (1m)	▽ Lavender #584
2 (1.9m)	■ Purple #596
1 (1m)	♡ Honey gold #645
1 (1m)	⊘ True blue #822
1 (1m)	★ Olympic blue #849
3 (2.8m)	Uncoded areas are black #12 Continental Stitches
	╱ Black #12 Straight Stitch and Overcasting
	╱ Honey gold #645 Backstitch and Straight Stitch
	Fine #8 Braid
4 (3.7m)	╱ Grapefruit #052F (1-strand) Straight Stitch
	╱ Grapefruit #052F (2-strands) Backstitch and Straight Stitch

Color numbers given are for Coats & Clark Red Heart Classic worsted weight yarn Art. #267 and Kreinik Fine (#8) Braid.

Bat

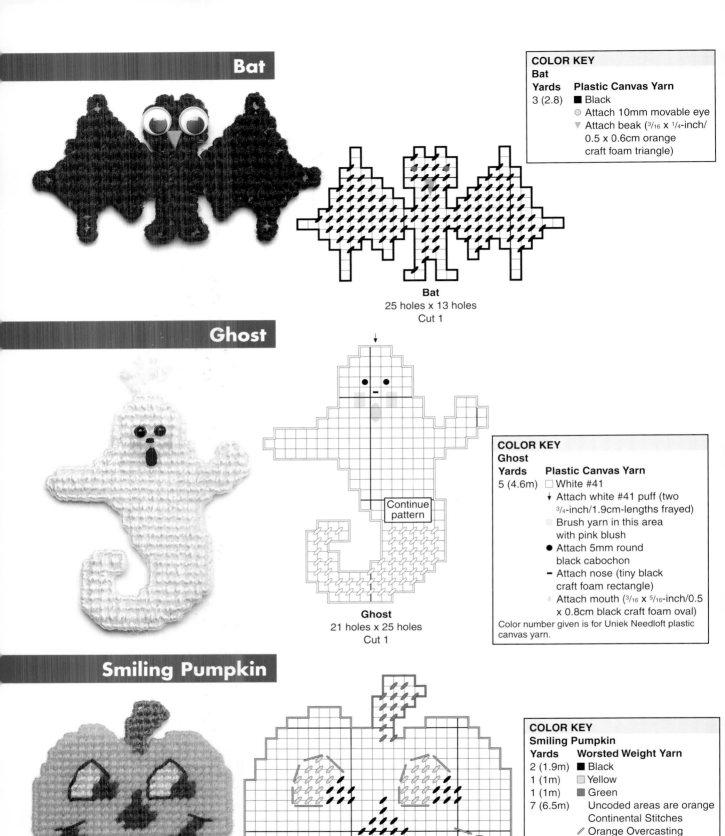

Bat
25 holes x 13 holes
Cut 1

Ghost

Continue pattern

Ghost
21 holes x 25 holes
Cut 1

Smiling Pumpkin

Smiling Pumpkin
25 holes x 25 holes
Cut 1

112

Peek-a-Boo Pumpkin

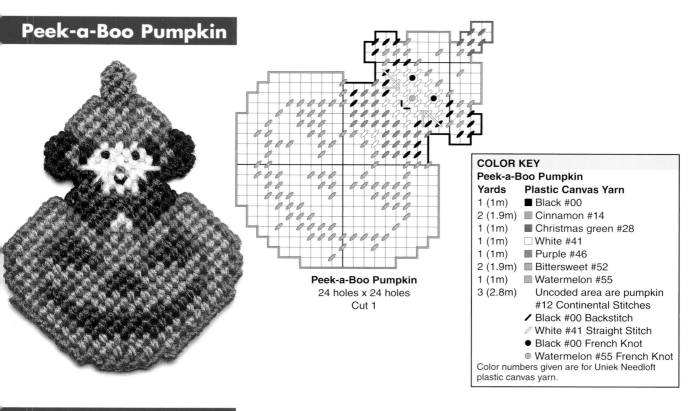

Peek-a-Boo Pumpkin
24 holes x 24 holes
Cut 1

COLOR KEY
Peek-a-Boo Pumpkin

Yards	Plastic Canvas Yarn
1 (1m)	■ Black #00
2 (1.9m)	▨ Cinnamon #14
1 (1m)	■ Christmas green #28
1 (1m)	☐ White #41
1 (1m)	▨ Purple #46
2 (1.9m)	▨ Bittersweet #52
1 (1m)	▨ Watermelon #55
3 (2.8m)	Uncoded area are pumpkin #12 Continental Stitches
	╱ Black #00 Backstitch
	╱ White #41 Straight Stitch
	● Black #00 French Knot
	● Watermelon #55 French Knot

Color numbers given are for Uniek Needloft plastic canvas yarn.

Spooky Characters

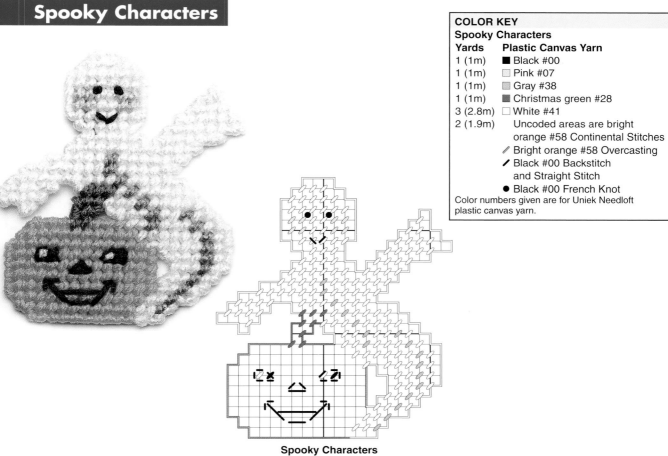

Spooky Characters
22 holes x 25 holes
Cut 1

COLOR KEY
Spooky Characters

Yards	Plastic Canvas Yarn
1 (1m)	■ Black #00
1 (1m)	☐ Pink #07
1 (1m)	▨ Gray #38
1 (1m)	■ Christmas green #28
3 (2.8m)	☐ White #41
2 (1.9m)	Uncoded areas are bright orange #58 Continental Stitches
	╱ Bright orange #58 Overcasting
	╱ Black #00 Backstitch and Straight Stitch
	● Black #00 French Knot

Color numbers given are for Uniek Needloft plastic canvas yarn.

Santa Claus

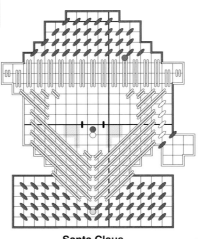

Santa Claus
18 holes x 21 holes
Cut 1

Mrs. Claus

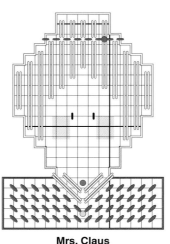

Mrs. Claus
15 holes x 21 holes
Cut 1

Santa in the Chimney

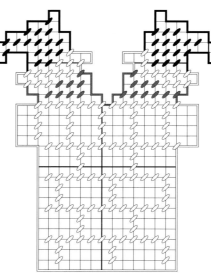

Santa in the Chimney
21 holes x 25 holes
Cut 1

Gingerbread Boy

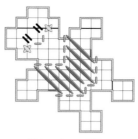

Gingerbread Boy
12 holes x 12 holes
Cut 1

Gingerbread Girl

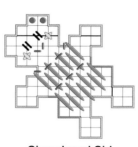

Gingerbread Girl
12 holes x 12 holes
Cut 1

Lamppost Noel

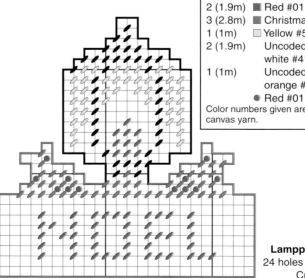

Lamppost Noel
24 holes x 25 holes
Cut 1

Reindeer

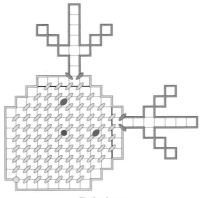

Reindeer
18 holes x 18 holes
Cut 1

Jingle Bell Reindeer

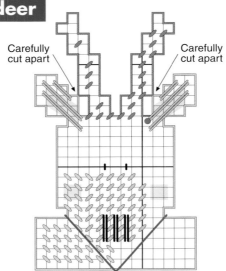

Carefully cut apart

Carefully cut apart

Jingle Bell Reindeer
15 holes x 25 holes
Cut 1

Mini Christmas Tree

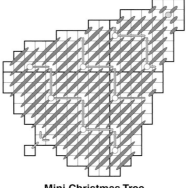

Mini Christmas Tree
17 holes x 17 holes
Cut 1 from green plastic canvas

Jolly St. Nick

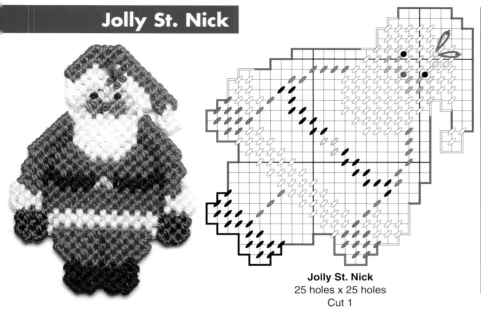

Jolly St. Nick
25 holes x 25 holes
Cut 1

Welcoming Santa

Illustration on page 168

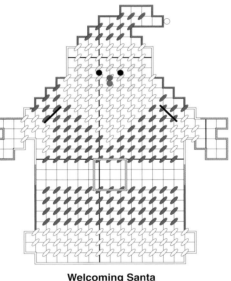

Welcoming Santa
22 holes x 25 holes
Cut 1

Christmas Bell

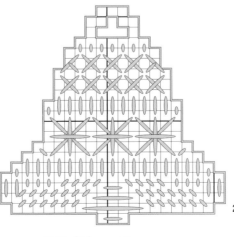

Christmas Bell
21 holes x 21 holes
Cut 1

Waving Santa

Illustrations on page 168

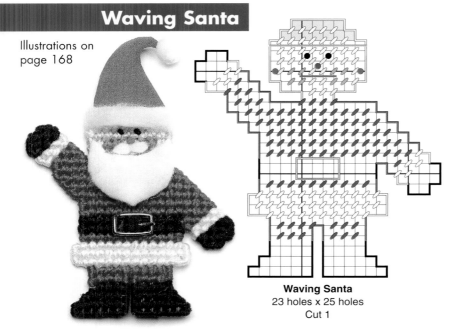

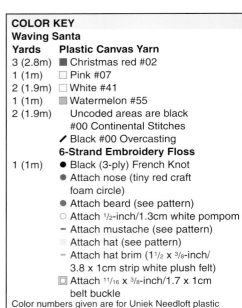

Waving Santa
23 holes x 25 holes
Cut 1

COLOR KEY
Waving Santa

Yards	Plastic Canvas Yarn
3 (2.8m)	■ Christmas red #02
1 (1m)	☐ Pink #07
2 (1.9m)	☐ White #41
1 (1m)	▨ Watermelon #55
2 (1.9m)	Uncoded areas are black #00 Continental Stitches
	╱ Black #00 Overcasting

6-Strand Embroidery Floss

1 (1m)	● Black (3-ply) French Knot
	● Attach nose (tiny red craft foam circle)
	● Attach beard (see pattern)
	○ Attach ½-inch/1.3cm white pompom
	▬ Attach mustache (see pattern)
	▢ Attach hat (see pattern)
	▬ Attach hat brim (1½ x ⅜-inch/ 3.8 x 1cm strip white plush felt)
	▢ Attach ¹¹⁄₁₆ x ⅜-inch/1.7 x 1cm belt buckle

Color numbers given are for Uniek Needloft plastic canvas yarn.

Side-View Snowman

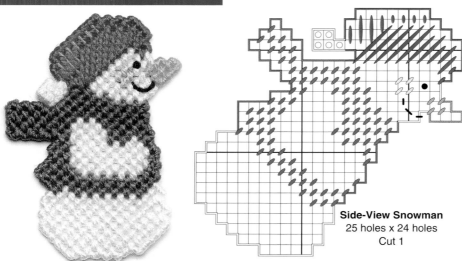

Side-View Snowman
25 holes x 24 holes
Cut 1

COLOR KEY
Side-View Snowman

Yards	Plastic Canvas Yarn
2 (1.9m)	■ Christmas red #02
1 (1m)	☐ Pink #07
2 (1.9m)	■ Christmas green #28
2 (1.9m)	■ Royal #32
1 (1m)	▨ Bright orange #58
4 (3.7m)	Uncoded areas are white #41 Continental Stitches
	╱ White #41 Overcasting
1 (1m)	╱ Black #00 Backstitch
	● Black #00 French Knot
	○ White #41 French Knot

Color numbers given are for Uniek Needloft plastic canvas yarn.

Red Santa Hat

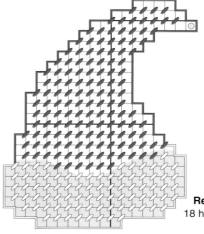

Red Santa Hat
18 holes x 22 holes
Cut 1

COLOR KEY
Red Santa Hat

Yards	Plastic Canvas Yarn
3 (2.8m)	■ Christmas red #02
2 (1.9m)	☐ White #41
	▢ Attach white faux fur
	○ Attach 1½-inch/3.8cm white pompom

Color numbers given are for Uniek Needloft plastic canvas yarn.

Blue Angel

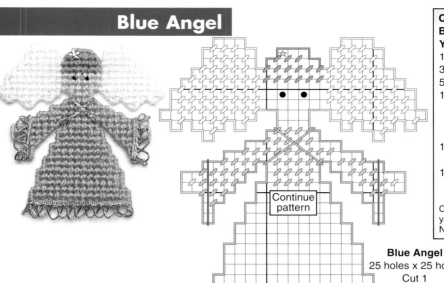

COLOR KEY
Blue Angel

Yards	Plastic Canvas Yarn
1 (1m)	▨ Rust #09
3 (2.8m)	☐ White #41
5 (4.6m)	▨ Bright blue #60
1 (1m)	Uncoded areas are pink #07 Continental Stitches
	∕ Pink #07 Overcasting

1/8-Inch/0.3cm Metallic Needlepoint Yarn

1 (1m)	∕ Silver #PC2 Straight Stitch

#8 Pearl Cotton

1 (1m)	● Black French Knot
	☆ Attach 7mm crystal faceted star
	▮ Attach 7/16-inch/1.1cm silver metallic trim

Color numbers given are for Uniek Needloft plastic canvas yarn and Rainbow Gallery Plastic Canvas 7 Metallic Needlepoint Yarn.

Continue pattern

Blue Angel
25 holes x 25 holes
Cut 1

Angel With Charm

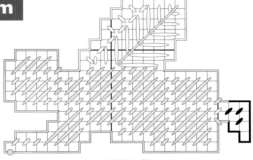

Angel With Charm
23 holes x 15 holes
Cut 1

COLOR KEY
Angel With Charm

Yards	Plastic Canvas Yarn
1 (1m)	■ Black #00
2 (1.9m)	☐ Sail blue #35
1 (1m)	☐ White #41
1 (1m)	☐ Pale peach #56
1 (1m)	☐ Yellow #57
	∕ White #41 Straight Stitch
	○ Attach gold jump ring then 1/2-inch/8.9cm gold heart charm

Color numbers given are for Uniek Needloft plastic canvas yarn.

Holly Leaf

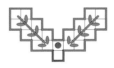

Holly Leaf
9 holes x 5 holes
Cut 1

COLOR KEY
Holly Leaf

Yards	Plastic Canvas Yarn
1 (1m)	▨ Holly #27
1 (1m)	∕ Christmas red #02 Overcasting
	∕ Holly #27 Straight Stitch
	● Christmas red #02 French Knot

Color numbers given are for Uniek Needloft plastic canvas yarn.

Christmas Bows

Red Christmas Bow
16 holes x 11 holes
Cut 1

Green Christmas Bow
16 holes x 11 holes
Cut 1

COLOR KEY
Red Christmas Bow

Yards	Plastic Canvas Yarn
2 (1.9m)	■ Christmas red #02
1 (1m)	▨ Burgundy #03

Color numbers given are for Uniek Needloft plastic canvas yarn.

COLOR KEY
Green Christmas Bow

Yards	Plastic Canvas Yarn
2 (1.9m)	☐ Moss #25
1 (1m)	■ Holly #27

Color numbers given are for Uniek Needloft plastic canvas yarn.

Christmas Angel

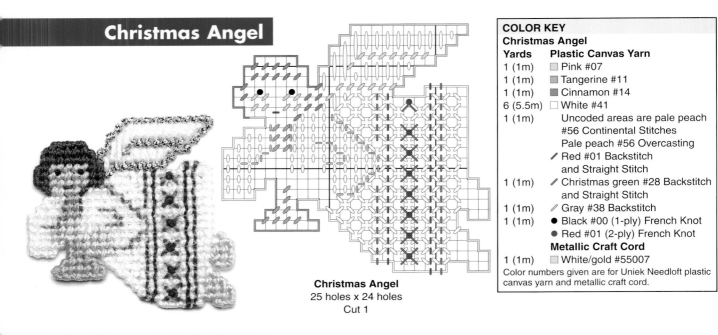

Christmas Angel
25 holes x 24 holes
Cut 1

COLOR KEY
Christmas Angel

Yards	Plastic Canvas Yarn
1 (1m)	Pink #07
1 (1m)	Tangerine #11
1 (1m)	Cinnamon #14
6 (5.5m)	White #41
1 (1m)	Uncoded areas are pale peach #56 Continental Stitches Pale peach #56 Overcasting
	Red #01 Backstitch and Straight Stitch
1 (1m)	Christmas green #28 Backstitch and Straight Stitch
1 (1m)	Gray #38 Backstitch
1 (1m)	● Black #00 (1-ply) French Knot
	● Red #01 (2-ply) French Knot

Metallic Craft Cord

1 (1m)	White/gold #55007

Color numbers given are for Uniek Needloft plastic canvas yarn and metallic craft cord.

Santa Face

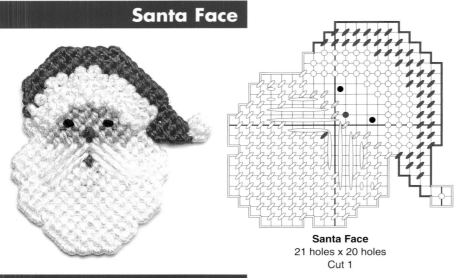

Santa Face
21 holes x 20 holes
Cut 1

COLOR KEY
Santa Face

Yards	Plastic Canvas Yarn
2 (1.9m)	Christmas red #02
1 (1m)	Pink #07
6 (5.5m)	White #41
1 (1m)	Uncoded areas are pale peach #56 Continental Stitches
1 (1m)	● Black #00 French Knot
	● Christmas red #02 French Knot
	○ White #41 French Knot

Color numbers given are for Uniek Needloft plastic canvas yarn.

Candy Cane

Candy Cane
11 holes x 21 holes
Cut 1

COLOR KEY
Candy Cane

Yards	Plastic Canvas Yarn
2 (1.9m)	White #41
2 (1.9m)	Watermelon #55

Color numbers given are for Uniek Needloft plastic canvas yarn.

Christmas Horn

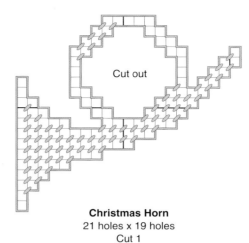

Christmas Horn
21 holes x 19 holes
Cut 1

COLOR KEY
Christmas Horn
Yards	Plastic Canvas Yarn
4 (3.7m)	▢ Tangerine #11

Color number given is for Uniek
Needloft plastic canvas yarn.

Gold Bead Ornament

COLOR KEY
Gold Bead Ornament
Yards	Plastic Canvas Yarn
1 (1m)	▢ Tangerine #11
2 (1.9m)	▣ Watermelon #55
2 (1.9m)	■ Bright purple #64

⅛-Inch/0.3cm Metallic Needlepoint Yarn
1 (1m)	▢ Gold #PC1
	○ Attach 4mm gold bead on gold #PC1 hanger
	↑ Attach 4mm gold bead tassel (3 strings of 8 to 9 beads)

Color numbers given are for Uniek Needloft plastic canvas
yarn and Rainbow Gallery Plastic Canvas 7 Metallic
Needlepoint Yarn.

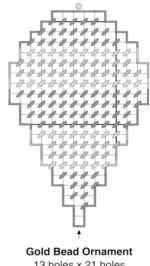

Gold Bead Ornament
13 holes x 21 holes
Cut 1

Gold Star Ornament

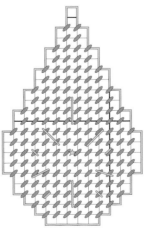
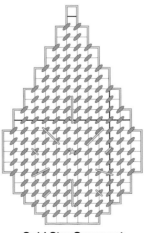

Gold Star Ornament
13 holes x 21 holes
Cut 1

COLOR KEY
Gold Star Ornament
Yards	Plastic Canvas Yarn
3 (2.8m)	■ Bright purple #64

⅛-Inch/0.3cm Metallic Needlepoint Yarn
2 (1.9m)	⁄ Gold #PC1 Straight Stitch and Overcasting
	☆ Attach 25mm gold star

Color numbers given are for Uniek Needloft plastic canvas
yarn and Rainbow Gallery Plastic Canvas 7 Metallic
Needlepoint Yarn.

Red Bead Ornament

COLOR KEY
Red Bead Ornament

Yards	Plastic Canvas Yarn
2 (1.9m)	■ Christmas red #02
1 (1m)	☐ White #41
2 (1.9m)	Uncoded areas are fern #23 Continental Stitches
	⁄ Fern #23 Overcasting
	↓ Attach 8mm red wooden bead on ¹⁄₁₆-inch/0.2cm-wide red satin ribbon hanger
	● Attach 8mm red wooden bead on 4 strands ¹⁄₁₆-inch/0.2cm-wide red satin ribbon tail

Color numbers given are for Uniek Needloft plastic canvas yarn.

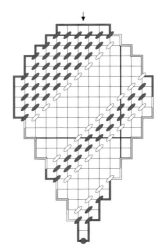

Red Bead Ornament
13 holes x 21 holes
Cut 1

Pink Roses Ornament

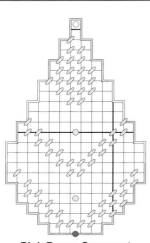

Pink Roses Ornament
13 holes x 21 holes
Cut 1

COLOR KEY
Pink Roses Ornament

Yards	Plastic Canvas Yarn
3 (2.8m)	☐ Pink #07
2 (1.9m)	Uncoded background is white #41 Continental Stitches
	⁄ White #41 Overcasting
	○ Attach white #41 hanger
	○ Attach ³⁄₈-inch/1cm pink ribbon rose with leaves
	● Attach 1³⁄₄-inch/4.4cm white tassel

Color numbers given are for Uniek Needloft plastic canvas yarn.

Red Rhinestone Ornament

COLOR KEY
Red Rhinestone Ornament

Yards	Plastic Canvas Yarn
2 (1.9m)	■ Christmas red #02
2 (1.9m)	Uncoded background is holly #27 Continental Stitches
	⁄ Holly #27 Overcasting
	¹⁄₈-Inch/0.3cm Metallic Needlepoint Yarn
1 (1m)	☐ Gold #PC1
	↓ Attach gold #PC1 hanger
	● Attach 7mm round ruby faceted stone
	● Attach 5mm round ruby faceted stone
	● Attach 1³⁄₄-inch/4.4cm red tassel

Color numbers given are for Uniek Needloft plastic canvas yarn and Rainbow Gallery Plastic Canvas 7 Metallic Needlepoint Yarn.

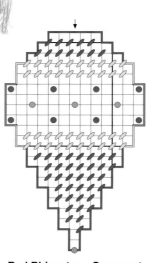

Red Rhinestone Ornament
13 holes x 21 holes
Cut 1

By the Sea

Celebrate the beauty of the sea by stitching these tiny nautical motifs.

Frilled Dogwinkle

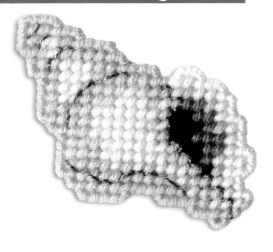

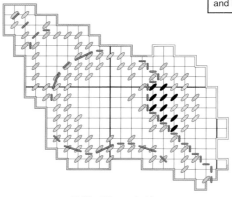

Frilled Dogwinkle
21 holes x 18 holes
Cut 1

Basket Cockle

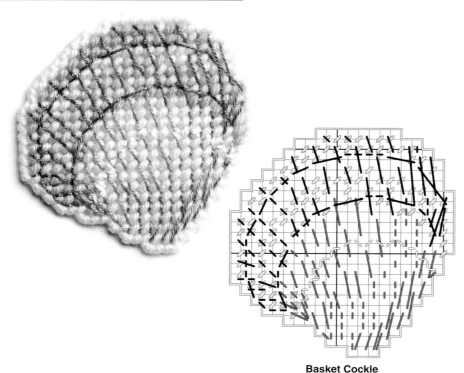

Basket Cockle
21 holes x 22 holes
Cut 1

Sand Dollar

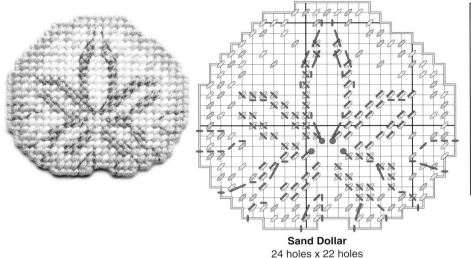

Sand Dollar
24 holes x 22 holes
Cut 1

COLOR KEY
Sand Dollar

Yards	Worsted Weight Yarn
1 (1m)	▨ Tan #334
4 (3.7m)	☐ Silver #412
4 (3.7m)	Uncoded background is eggshell #111 Continental Stitches
	#5 Pearl Cotton
2 (1.9m)	✐ Medium beaver gray #647 Backstitch and Straight Stitch
	● Medium beaver gray #647 French Knot

Color numbers given are for Coats & Clark Red Heart Classic worsted weight yarn Art. E267 and DMC #5 pearl cotton.

Rough Keyhole Limpet

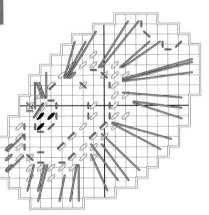

Rough Keyhole Limpet
19 holes x 19 holes
Cut 1

COLOR KEY
Rough Keyhole Limpet

Yards	Worsted Weight Yarn
1 (1m)	■ Black #12
2 (1.9m)	▨ Coffee #365
1 (1m)	☐ Silver #412
4 (3.7m)	Uncoded background is eggshell #111 Continental Stitches
	⁄ Eggshell #111 Straight Stitch and Overcasting
	⁄ Coffee #365 Straight Stitch
	#5 Pearl Cotton
1 (1m)	✐ Ultra dark beaver gray #844 Backstitch and Straight Stitch

Color numbers given are for Coats & Clark Red Heart Classic worsted weight yarn Art. E267 and DMC #5 pearl cotton.

Pink Scallop

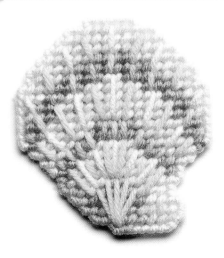

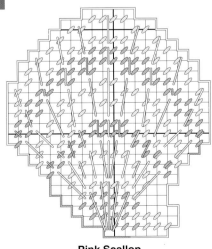

Pink Scallop
19 holes x 22 holes
Cut 1

COLOR KEY
Pink Scallop

Yards	Worsted Weight Yarn
2 (1.9m)	☐ Sea coral #246
1 (1m)	▨ Tan #334
2 (1.9m)	☐ Lily pink #719
2 (1.9m)	▨ Pale rose #755
4 (3.7m)	Uncoded background is eggshell #111 Continental Stitches
	⁄ Eggshell #111 Straight Stitch and Overcasting
	⁄ Sea coral #246 Straight Stitch
	⁄ Tan #334 Straight Stitch

Color numbers given are for Coats & Clark Red Heart Classic worsted weight yarn Art. E267.

Seagull

Seagull
24 holes x 24 holes
Cut 1

Sand Castle

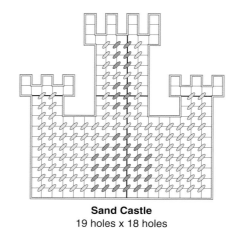

Sand Castle
19 holes x 18 holes
Cut 1

Sand Bucket & Shovel

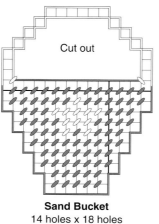

Cut out

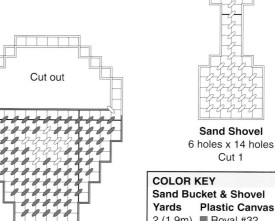

Sand Shovel
6 holes x 14 holes
Cut 1

Sand Bucket
14 holes x 18 holes
Cut 1

Dolphin

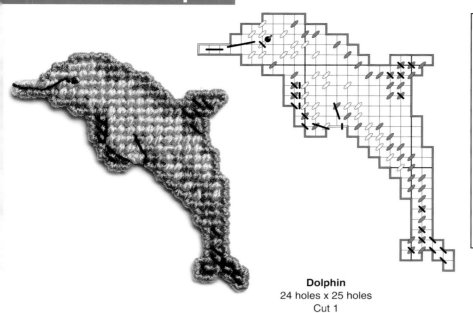

Dolphin
24 holes x 25 holes
Cut 1

Whale

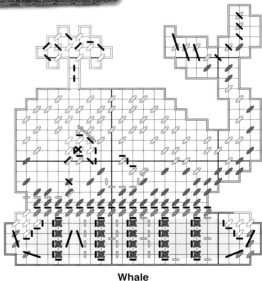

Whale
24 holes x 25 holes
Cut 1

Flip-Flop Sandal

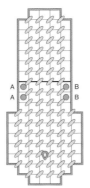

Flip-Flop Sandal
7 holes x 17 holes
Cut 1

Colorful Beach Ball

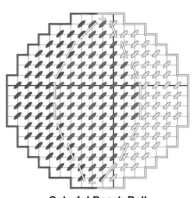

Colorful Beach Ball
17 holes x 17 holes
Cut 1

Bouncing Beach Ball

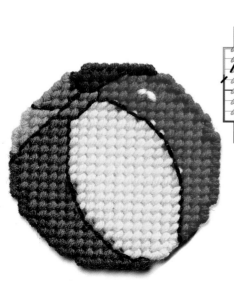

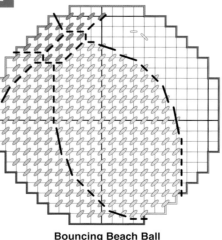

Bouncing Beach Ball
21 holes x 21 holes
Cut 1

Colorful Kite

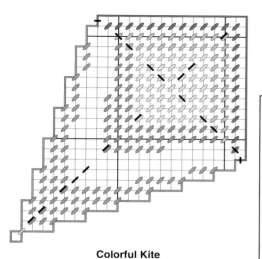

Colorful Kite
22 holes x 22 holes
Cut 1

Wind Sock

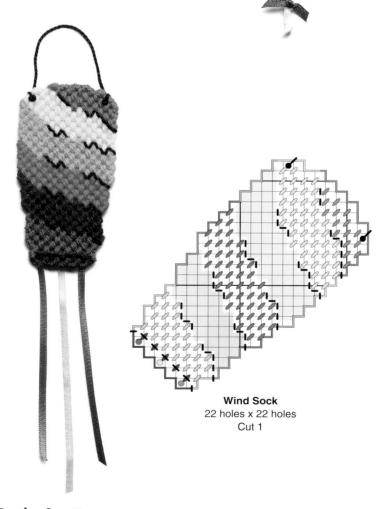

Wind Sock
22 holes x 22 holes
Cut 1

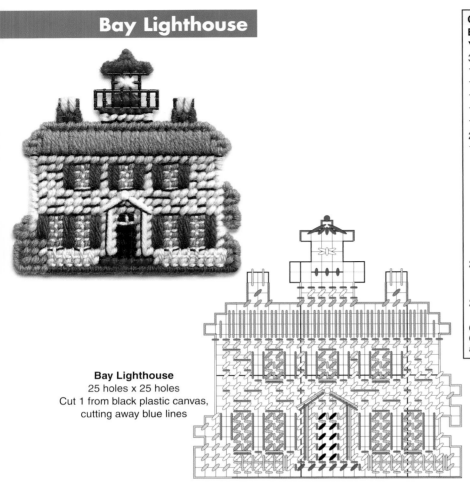

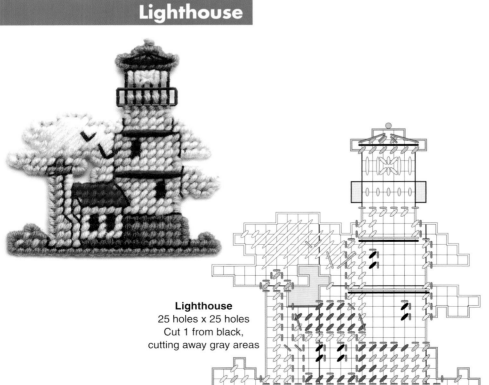

COLOR KEY
Bay Lighthouse

Yards	Worsted Weight Yarn
3 (2.8m)	☐ Off-white #3
1 (1m)	■ Black #12
1 (1m)	▦ Mid brown #339
1 (1m)	▨ Nickel #401
1 (1m)	☐ Silver #412
1 (1m)	☐ Light sage #631
2 (1.9m)	▤ Country blue #882
1 (1m)	■ Country red #914
	⁄ Off-white #3 Straight Stitch
	⁄ Mid brown #339 Straight Stitch
	⁄ Silver #412 Straight Stitch
	⁄ Country blue #882 Straight Stitch
	⁄ Country red #914 Backstitch
	○ Off-white #3 French Knot
	● Country red #914 French Knot

#3 Pearl Cotton

Yards	
2 (1.9m)	⁄ Light beige gray #822 Backstitch and Straight Stitch

#5 Pearl Cotton

Yards	
2 (1.9m)	⁄ Black #310 Backstitch and Straight Stitch

Color numbers given are for Coats & Clark Red Heart Classic worsted weight yarn Art. E267 and DMC #3 and #5 pearl cotton.

Bay Lighthouse
25 holes x 25 holes
Cut 1 from black plastic canvas,
cutting away blue lines

COLOR KEY
Lighthouse

Yards	Worsted Weight Yarn
4 (3.7m)	☐ Off-white #03
1 (1m)	■ Black #12
1 (1m)	☐ Maize #261
2 (1.9m)	▨ Nickel #401
2 (1.9m)	☐ Silver #412
1 (1m)	■ Windsor blue #808
1 (1m)	■ Country red #914
	Uncoded areas are off-white #3 Continental Stitches
	⁄ Black #12 Straight Stitch
	⁄ Nickel #401 Backstitch
	⁄ Country red #914 (2-ply) Straight Stitch
	○ Nickel #401 (2-wrap) French Knot

#5 Pearl Cotton

Yards	
3 (2.8m)	⁄ Black (1-strand) Backstitch and Straight Stitch
	⁄ Black (2-strand) Backstitch

Color numbers given are for Coats & Clark Red Heart Classic worsted weight yarn Art. E267.

Lighthouse
25 holes x 25 holes
Cut 1 from black,
cutting away gray areas

Antique Glass Float

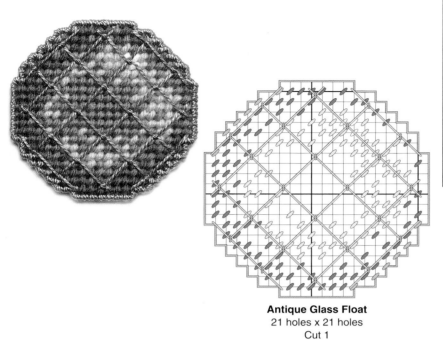

Antique Glass Float
21 holes x 21 holes
Cut 1

Thomas Point Shoal Lighthouse

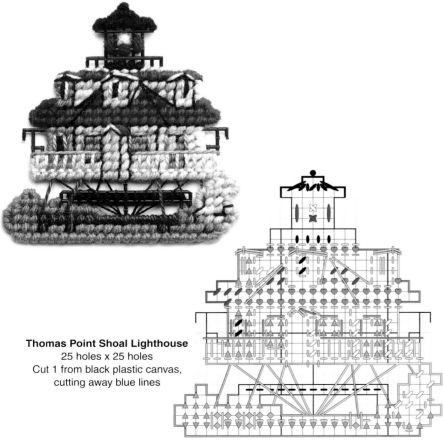

Thomas Point Shoal Lighthouse
25 holes x 25 holes
Cut 1 from black plastic canvas,
cutting away blue lines

Fantasy Fish

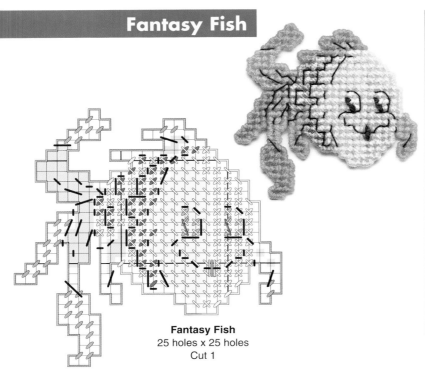

Fantasy Fish
25 holes x 25 holes
Cut 1

COLOR KEY
Fantasy Fish

Yards	Plastic Canvas Yarn
1 (1m)	☐ White #41
1 (1m)	☐ Yellow #57
1 (1m)	☐ Bright blue #60
1 (1m)	■ Bright green #61
3 (2.8m)	■ Bright pink #62
2 (1.9m)	Uncoded areas with peach background are bright orange #58 Continental Stitches
2 (1.9m)	Uncoded area under pearl Straight Stitches with pale yellow background is bright yellow #63 Continental Stitches
	╱ Bright orange #58 Overcasting
	╱ Bright yellow #63 Overcasting
1 (1m)	╱ Black #00 (1-strand) Straight Stitch
	╱ Black #00 (2-strand) Straight Stitch
	╱ Bright pink #62 (1-ply) Straight Stitch

Tapestry #12 Braid

3 (2.8m)	╱ Pearl #032 (1-strand) Straight Stitch
	╱ Pearl #032 (2-strand) Straight Stitch

#8 Pearl Cotton

2 (1.9m)	╱ Black Backstitch and Straight Stitch

Color numbers given are for Uniek Needloft plastic canvas yarn and Kreinik Medium (#12) Tapestry Braid.

Orange Fish

COLOR KEY
Orange Fish

Yards	Plastic Canvas Yarn
4 (3.7m)	☐ Tangerine #11
1 (1m)	☐ White #41
1 (1m)	■ Turquoise #54
	Uncoded areas are tangerine #11 Continental Stitches
1 (1m)	╱ Black #00 Straight Stitch

Color numbers given are for Uniek Needloft plastic canvas yarn.

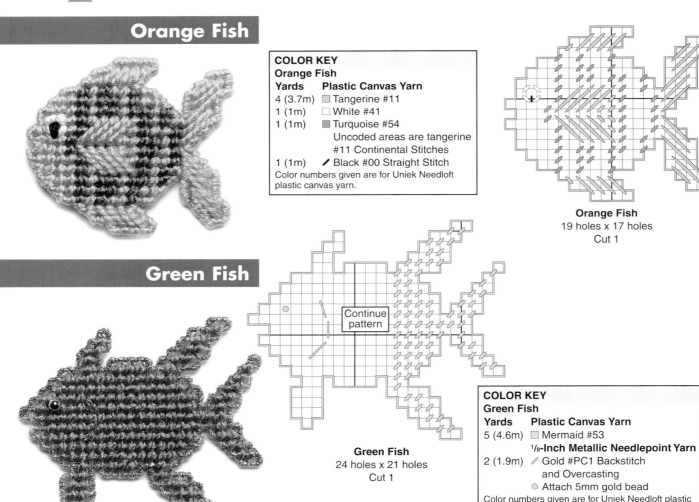

Orange Fish
19 holes x 17 holes
Cut 1

Green Fish

Continue pattern

Green Fish
24 holes x 21 holes
Cut 1

COLOR KEY
Green Fish

Yards	Plastic Canvas Yarn
5 (4.6m)	☐ Mermaid #53

1/8-Inch Metallic Needlepoint Yarn

2 (1.9m)	╱ Gold #PC1 Backstitch and Overcasting
	○ Attach 5mm gold bead

Color numbers given are for Uniek Needloft plastic canvas yarn and Rainbow Gallery Plastic Canvas 7 Metallic Needlepoint Yarn.

Royal Sand Castle

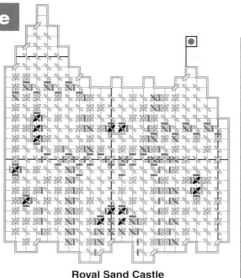

Royal Sand Castle
21 holes x 25 holes
Cut 1 from almond plastic canvas,
cutting away blue lines

Sailboat

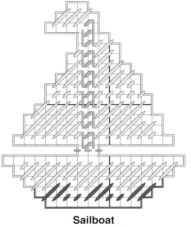

Sailboat
17 holes x 20 holes
Cut 1

Anchor

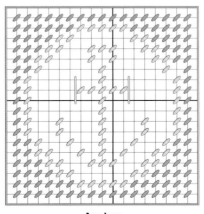

Anchor
18 holes x 19 holes
Cut 1

Starfish

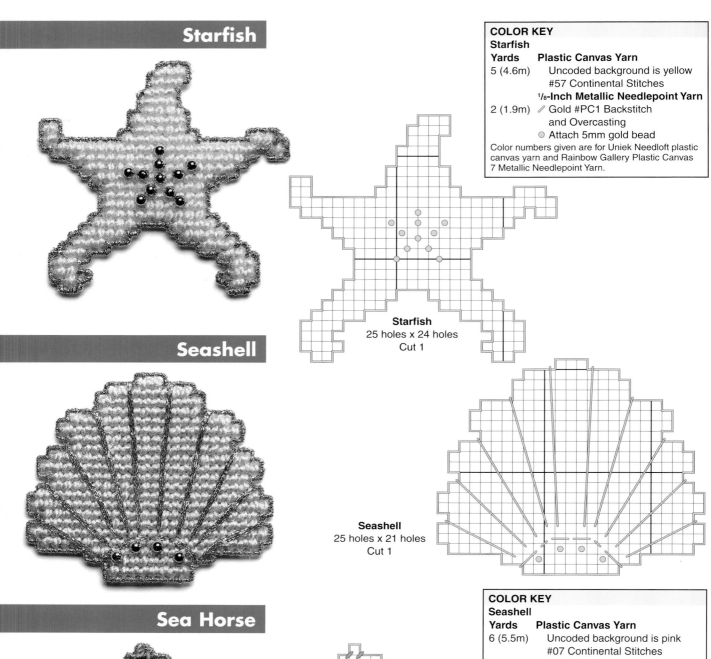

Starfish
25 holes x 24 holes
Cut 1

Seashell

Seashell
25 holes x 21 holes
Cut 1

Sea Horse

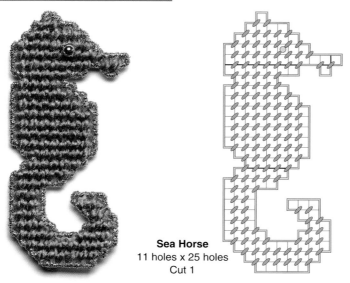

Sea Horse
11 holes x 25 holes
Cut 1

Pink Flamingo

Illustration on page 169

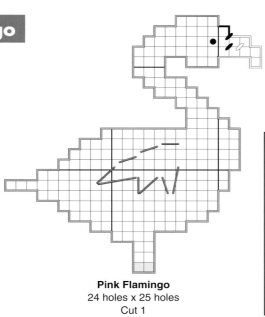

Pink Flamingo
24 holes x 25 holes
Cut 1

COLOR KEY

Pink Flamingo

Yards	Plastic Canvas Yarn
1 (1m)	■ Black #00
1 (1m)	□ White #41
5 (4.6m)	Uncoded area is bright pink #62 Continental Stitches
	⁄ Bright pink #62 Overcasting

#3 Pearl Cotton

1 (1m)	⁄ Black Backstitch
	● Attach 5mm black cabochon
	▪ Attach legs (see pattern)

Color numbers given are for Uniek Needloft plastic canvas yarn.

Lobster

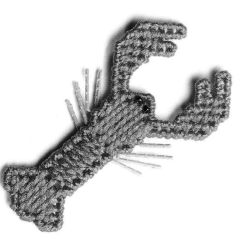

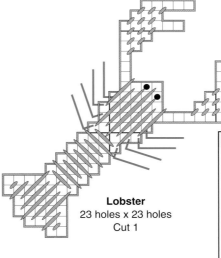

Lobster
23 holes x 23 holes
Cut 1

COLOR KEY

Lobster

Yards	Plastic Canvas Yarn
5 (4.6m)	▨ Rust #09
	● Attach 3mm round black bead
	∟ Attach ³⁄₄-inch/1.9cm-long L-shaped pieces tan plastic canvas

Color number given is for Uniek Needloft plastic canvas yarn.

Crab

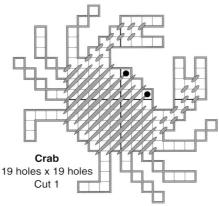

Crab
19 holes x 19 holes
Cut 1

COLOR KEY

Crab

Yards	Plastic Canvas Yarn
5 (4.6m)	▨ Bittersweet #52
	● Attach 3mm round black bead

Color number given is for Uniek Needloft plastic canvas yarn.

Munchies

This delicious collection of motifs is sure to make your mouth water!

rawberry Ice-Cream Cone

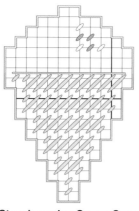

Strawberry Ice-Cream Cone
12 holes x 19 holes
Cut 1

COLOR KEY
Strawberry Ice-Cream Cone

Yards	Plastic Canvas Yarn
1 (1m)	▨ Lavender #05
1 (1m)	☐ White #41
2 (1.9m)	Uncoded areas are pink #07 Continental Stitches
	✎ Pink #07 Overcasting
	Worsted Weight Yarn
3 (2.8m)	☐ Buff #334
	✎ Buff #334 Straight Stitch

Color numbers given are for Uniek Needloft plastic canvas yarn and Coats & Clark Red Heart Super Saver worsted weight yarn Art. E300.

Double-Dip Sundae

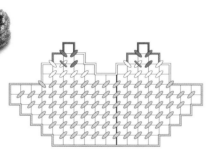

Double-Dip Sundae
18 holes x 10 holes
Cut 1

COLOR KEY
Double-Dip Sundae

Yards	Plastic Canvas Yarn
1 (1m)	■ Brown #15
2 (1.9m)	▨ Sail blue #35
1 (1m)	☐ White #41
1 (1m)	✎ Red #01 Overcasting
	✎ Brown #15 Straight Stitch

Color numbers given are for Uniek Needloft plastic canvas yarn.

Chocolate Milk Shake

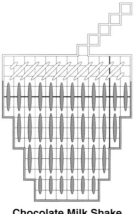

Chocolate Milk Shake
12 holes x 19 holes
Cut 1

COLOR KEY
Chocolate Milk Shake

Yards	Plastic Canvas Yarn
2 (1.9m)	☐ White #41
	Worsted Weight Yarn
3 (2.8m)	■ Taupe #2335

Color numbers given are for Uniek Needloft plastic canvas yarn and Coats & Clark Red Heart TLC Essentials worsted weight yarn Art. E514.

Chocolate Chip Cookie

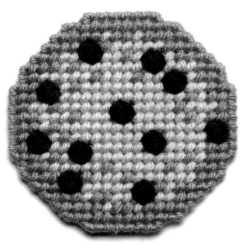

Chocolate Chip Cookie
21 holes x 21 holes
Cut 1

COLOR KEY
Chocolate Chip Cookie

Yards		Worsted Weight Yarn
3 (2.8m)		Warm brown #336
3 (2.8m)		Coffee #365 (2 strands)
3 (2.8m)		Coffee #365 (1 strand)

Uncoded background is tan #334 Continental Stitches
Color numbers given are for Coats & Clark Red Heart Classic worsted weight yarn Art. E267.

Cupcake

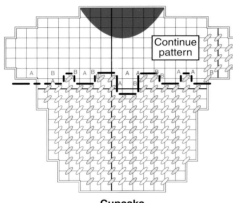

Continue pattern

Cupcake
22 holes x 18 holes
Cut 1

COLOR KEY
Cupcake

Yards		Plastic Canvas Yarn
3 (2.8m)		Pink #07
2 (1.9m)		Silver #37
2 (1.9m)		White #41

Pink #07 twisted loop (up at A, down at B)

6-Strand Embroidery Floss

1 (1m)	╱ Black (2-ply) Backstitch
	● Attach artificial cherry with stem (split open at bottom)

Color numbers given are for Uniek Needloft plastic canvas yarn.

Deep-Dish Pie

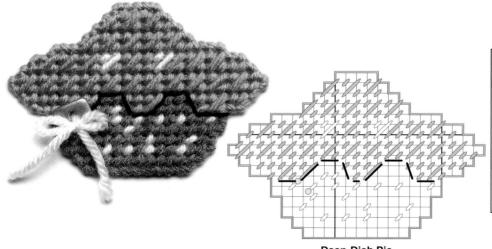

Deep-Dish Pie
24 holes x 16 holes
Cut 1

COLOR KEY
Deep-Dish Pie

Yards		Worsted Weight Yarn
4 (3.7m)		Medium brown
1 (1m)		Off-white
2 (1.9m)		Uncoded area is denim heather Continental Stitches
	╱	Denim heather Overcasting
	○	Attach silver button with off-white yarn bow

#3 Pearl Cotton

1 (1m)	╱ Black Backstitch

Ice-Cream Cone

COLOR KEY
Ice-Cream Cone

Yards	Plastic Canvas Yarn
1 (1m)	☐ Pink #07
1 (1m)	☐ Tangerine #11
2 (1.9m)	☐ Eggshell #39
2 (1.9m)	☐ Camel #43
1 (1m)	⟋ Black #00 (1-ply) Overcasting
	6-Strand Embroidery Floss
1 (1m)	⟋ Black (3-ply) Backstitch
	● Attach 8mm red bead

Color numbers given are for Uniek Needloft plastic canvas yarn.

Ice-Cream Bar

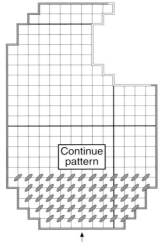

Continue pattern

Ice-Cream Bar
14 holes x 22 holes
Cut 1

COLOR KEY
Ice-Cream Bar

Yards	Plastic Canvas Yarn
5 (4.6m)	☐ Brown #15
1 (1m)	⟋ Eggshell #39 Overcasting
	⤴ Attach wooden craft stick

Color numbers given are for Uniek Needloft plastic canvas yarn.

Ice-Cream Cone
17 holes x 25 holes
Cut 1

Ice-Cream Sundae

COLOR KEY
Ice-Cream Sundae

Yards	Plastic Canvas Yarn
1 (1m)	■ Christmas red #02
2 (1.9m)	■ Brown #15
3 (2.8m)	☐ Moss #25
2 (1.9m)	Uncoded area is pink #07 Continental Stitches
	⟋ Pink #07 Overcasting
1 (1m)	⟋ White #41 Straight Stitch
	#3 Pearl Cotton
1 (1m)	⟋ Black Backstitch

Color numbers given are for Uniek Needloft plastic canvas yarn.

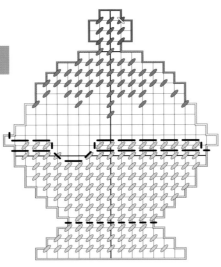

Ice-Cream Sundae
20 holes x 24 holes
Cut 1

Asparagus

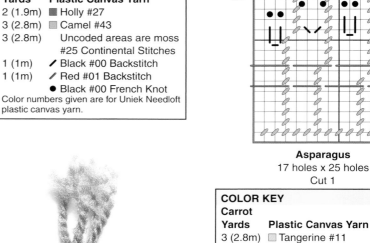

Asparagus
17 holes x 25 holes
Cut 1

COLOR KEY
Asparagus
Yards	Plastic Canvas Yarn
2 (1.9m)	■ Holly #27
3 (2.8m)	▢ Camel #43
3 (2.8m)	Uncoded areas are moss #25 Continental Stitches
1 (1m)	✏ Black #00 Backstitch
1 (1m)	✏ Red #01 Backstitch
	● Black #00 French Knot

Color numbers given are for Uniek Needloft plastic canvas yarn.

Carrot

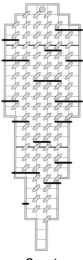

Carrot
7 holes x 24 holes
Cut 1

COLOR KEY
Carrot
Yards	Plastic Canvas Yarn
3 (2.8m)	▢ Tangerine #11
	◉ Attach fern #23 carrot top (thread two 6-inch/15.2cm lengths and tie in a knot)

6-Strand Embroidery Floss
1 (1m)	✏ Black (4-ply) Straight Stitch

Color numbers given are for Uniek Needloft plastic canvas yarn.

Cauliflower

COLOR KEY
Cauliflower
Yards	Plastic Canvas Yarn
1 (1m)	■ Black #00
2 (1.9m)	▢ Moss #25
1 (1m)	▨ Holly #27
5 (4.6m)	Uncoded areas are eggshell #39 Continental Stitches
	⁄ Eggshell #39 Overcasting
	✏ Black #00 Backstitch and Straight Stitch

Color numbers given are for Uniek Needloft plastic canvas yarn.

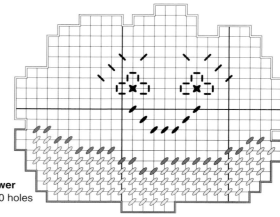

Cauliflower
25 holes x 20 holes
Cut 1

Pea Pod

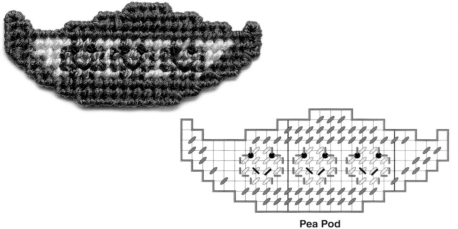

COLOR KEY
Pea Pod

Yards	Plastic Canvas Yarn
2 (1.9m)	☐ Moss #25
3 (2.8m)	■ Holly #27
1 (1m)	Uncoded background is bright green #61 Continental Stitches
1 (1m)	✦ Black #00 Backstitch
	✦ Holly #27 Backstitch
	● Black #00 French Knot

Color numbers given are for Uniek Needloft plastic canvas yarn.

Pea Pod
25 holes x 10 holes
Cut 1

Chili Pepper

COLOR KEY
Chili Pepper

Yards	Plastic Canvas Yarn
1 (1m)	■ Black #00
2 (1.9m)	■ Holly #27
1 (1m)	☐ White #41
3 (2.8m)	Uncoded areas are red #01 Continental Stitches
	✦ Red #01 Overcasting
	✦ Black #00 Backstitch and Straight Stitch
	⁄ White #41 Backstitch

Color numbers given are for Uniek Needloft plastic canvas yarn.

Chili Pepper
15 holes x 24 holes
Cut 1

Crunchy Carrots

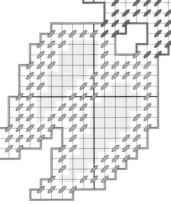

Crunchy Carrots
25 holes x 25 holes
Cut 1

COLOR KEY
Crunchy Carrots

Yards	Plastic Canvas Yarn
3 (2.8m)	■ Forest #29
3 (2.8m)	■ Bittersweet #52
2 (1.9m)	Uncoded areas with peach background are pumpkin #12 Continental Stitches
1 (1m)	Uncoded areas with green background are Christmas green #28 Continental Stitches

Color numbers given are for Uniek Needloft plastic canvas yarn.

Juicy Pear

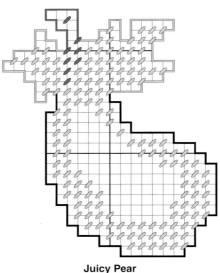

Juicy Pear
20 holes x 24 holes
Cut 1

COLOR KEY
Juicy Pear

Yards	Plastic Canvas Yarn
3 (2.8m)	☐ Tangerine #11
2 (1.9m)	☐ Christmas green #28
1 (1m)	■ Forest #29
2 (1.9m)	Uncoded areas are yellow #57 Continental Stitches

Color numbers given are for Uniek Needloft plastic canvas yarn.

Red Beet

COLOR KEY
Red Beet

Yards	Plastic Canvas Yarn
2 (1.9m)	☐ Christmas green #28
1 (1m)	■ Forest #29
2 (1.9m)	■ Bright purple #64
1 (1m)	Uncoded area is burgundy #03 Continental Stitches

Color numbers given are for Uniek Needloft plastic canvas yarn.

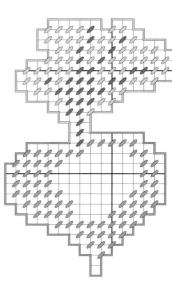

Red Beet
16 holes x 25 holes
Cut 1

Crisp Apple

Crisp Apple
20 holes x 22 holes
Cut 1

COLOR KEY
Crisp Apple

Yards	Plastic Canvas Yarn
2 (1.9m)	■ Burgundy #03
1 (1m)	☐ Christmas green #28
1 (1m)	■ Forest #29
2 (1.9m)	Uncoded areas are red #01 Continental Stitches

Color numbers given are for Uniek Needloft plastic canvas yarn.

Summer Corn

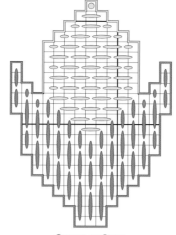

Summer Corn
15 holes x 22 holes
Cut 1

COLOR KEY
Summer Corn

Yards	Plastic Canvas Yarn
3 (2.8m)	■ Christmas green #28
3 (2.8m)	☐ Yellow #57 (2 strands)
	○ Yellow #57 (1-strand) Lark's Head Knot

Color numbers given are for Uniek Needloft plastic canvas yarn.

Harvest Corn

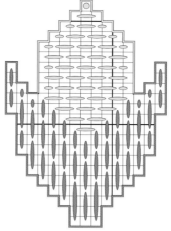

COLOR KEY
Harvest Corn

Yards	Plastic Canvas Yarn
1 (1m)	■ Burgundy #03 (2 strands)
1 (1m)	■ Rust #09 (2 strands)
1 (1m)	■ Brown #15 (2 strands)
2 (1.9m)	☐ Gold #17 (2 strands)
3 (2.8m)	☐ Beige #40 (1 strand)
	○ Beige #40 (1-strand) Lark's Head Knot

Color numbers given are for Uniek Needloft plastic canvas yarn.

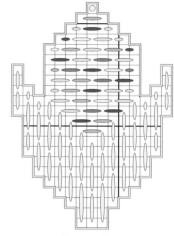

Harvest Corn
15 holes x 22 holes
Cut 1

Hamburger

Illustration on page 169

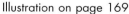

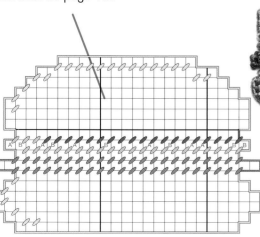

Hamburger
25 holes x 17 holes
Cut 1

COLOR KEY
Hamburger

Yards	Plastic Canvas Yarn
1 (1m)	■ Christmas red #02
1 (1m)	■ Cinnamon #14
2 (1.9m)	☐ Fern #23
1 (1m)	☐ Camel #41
5 (4.6m)	Uncoded areas are maple #13 Continental Stitches
	╱ Maple #13 Overcasting
	Fern #23 twisted loop (up at A, down at B)
	╲ Attach toothpick with pickle glued on (see pattern)

Color numbers given are for Uniek Needloft plastic canvas yarn.

■ **Munchies** ■

Cherries

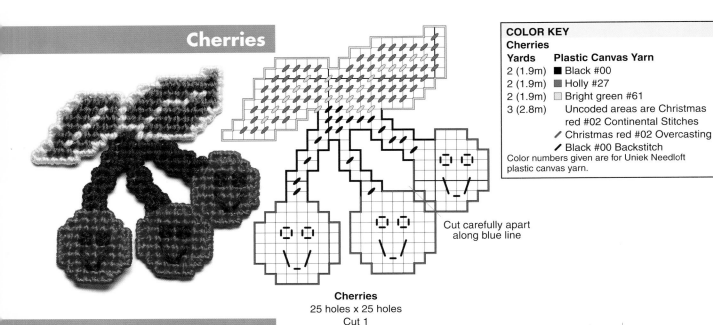

Cut carefully apart
along blue line

COLOR KEY
Cherries
Yards	Plastic Canvas Yarn
2 (1.9m)	■ Black #00
2 (1.9m)	■ Holly #27
2 (1.9m)	☐ Bright green #61
3 (2.8m)	Uncoded areas are Christmas red #02 Continental Stitches
	╱ Christmas red #02 Overcasting
	╱ Black #00 Backstitch

Color numbers given are for Uniek Needloft plastic canvas yarn.

Cherries
25 holes x 25 holes
Cut 1

Pear

Illustration on page 169

COLOR KEY
Pear
Yards	Plastic Canvas Yarn
1 (1m)	■ Burgundy #03
2 (1.9m)	☐ Tangerine #11
2 (1.9m)	☐ Lemon #20
1 (1m)	■ Fern #23 combined with burgundy #03
	Uncoded areas with peach background are combined tangerine #11 and lemon #20 Continental Stitches
2 (1.9m)	Uncoded area with pink background is watermelon #55 Continental Stitches
	╱ Fern #23 Overcasting
	╱ Watermelon #55 Overcasting
	↘ Attach leaf (see pattern)
	↓ Attach stem (natural twig)

Color numbers given are for Uniek Needloft plastic canvas yarn.

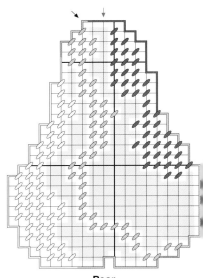

Pear
18 holes x 24 holes
Cut 1

Strawberry

Illustrations on page 169

COLOR KEY
Strawberry
Yards	Plastic Canvas Yarn
3 (2.8m)	■ Red #01
	● Attach black seed bead
	↓ Attach strawberry top (see patterns)

Color number given is for Uniek Needloft plastic canvas yarn.

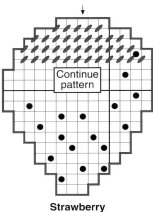

Continue pattern

Strawberry
14 holes x 17 holes
Cut 1

Apple

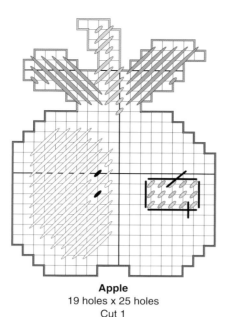

Apple
19 holes x 25 holes
Cut 1

Illustration on page 170

COLOR KEY
Apple

Yards	Worsted Weight Yarn
2 (1.9m)	☐ Off-white
2 (1.9m)	▨ Medium avocado green
1 (1m)	☐ Light brown
1 (1m)	☐ Gold
1 (1m)	☐ Country blue
1 (1m)	■ Black
4 (3.7m)	Uncoded areas are garnet Continental Stitches
	✎ Garnet Overcasting
	✎ Black Backstitch and Straight Stitch

Pineapple

COLOR KEY
Pineapple

Yards	Plastic Canvas Yarn
1 (1m)	▨ Rust #09
3 (2.8m)	Uncoded background below stem is tangerine #11 Continental Stitches
1 (1m)	✎ Cinnamon #14 Overcasting
	○ Attach 8mm topaz round cabochon
	☐ Attach tops (see pattern)

Color numbers given are for Uniek Needloft plastic canvas yarn.

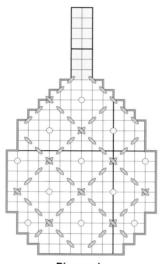

Pineapple
14 holes x 24 holes
Cut 1

Banana

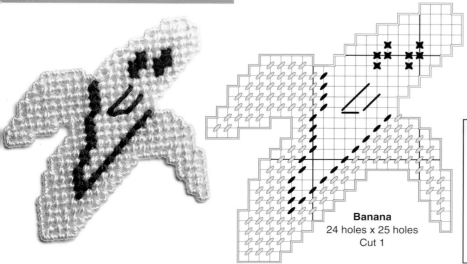

Banana
24 holes x 25 holes
Cut 1

COLOR KEY
Banana

Yards	Plastic Canvas Yarn
1 (1m)	■ Black #00
4 (3.7m)	☐ Yellow #57
2 (1.9m)	Uncoded background is lemon #20 Continental Stitches
	✎ Lemon #20 Overcasting
	✎ Black #00 Backstitch

Color numbers given are for Uniek Needloft plastic canvas yarn.

Flowered Teapot

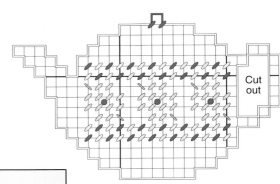

Flowered Teapot
25 holes x 16 holes
Cut 1

Gold-Rimmed Teacup

COLOR KEY
Flowered Teapot

Yards	Plastic Canvas Yarn
1 (1m)	■ Royal #32
1 (1m)	☐ Bright blue #60
1 (1m)	☐ Yellow #57
4 (3.7m)	Uncoded areas are white #41 Continental Stitches
	⁄ White #41 Overcasting
1 (1m)	⁄ Fern #23 Straight Stitch
	● Royal #32 French Knot

Color numbers given are for Uniek Needloft plastic canvas yarn.

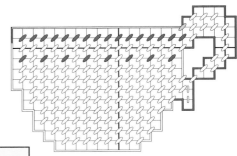

Gold-Rimmed Teacup
21 holes x 14 holes
Cut 1

COLOR KEY
Gold-Rimmed Teacup

Yards	Plastic Canvas Yarn
1 (1m)	■ Royal #32
3 (2.8m)	☐ White #41
	⁄ White #41 Backstitch

⅛-Inch/0.3cm Metallic Needlepoint Yarn

1 (1m)	☐ Gold #PC1

Color numbers given are for Uniek Needloft plastic canvas yarn and Rainbow Gallery Plastic Canvas 7 Metallic Needlepoint Yarn.

Delicate Teacup & Saucer

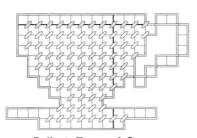

Delicate Teacup & Saucer
17 holes x 11 holes
Cut 1

COLOR KEY
Delicate Teacup & Saucer

Yards	Plastic Canvas Yarn
2 (1.9m)	☐ Pink #07
2 (1.9m)	☐ Bright blue #60

Color numbers given are for Uniek Needloft plastic canvas yarn.

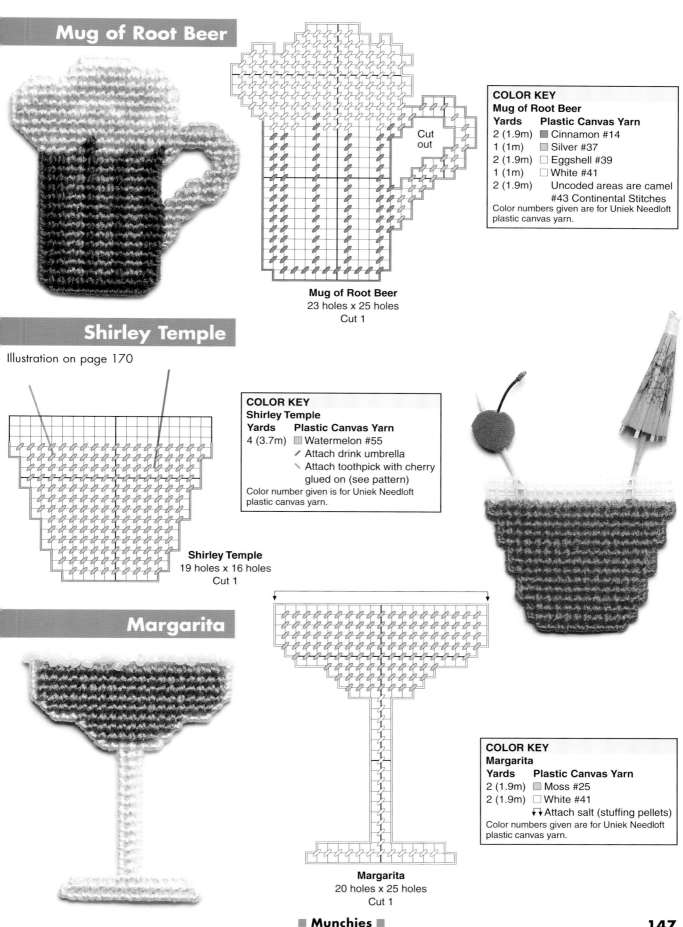

Mug of Root Beer

COLOR KEY
Mug of Root Beer
Yards	Plastic Canvas Yarn
2 (1.9m)	■ Cinnamon #14
1 (1m)	▨ Silver #37
2 (1.9m)	☐ Eggshell #39
1 (1m)	☐ White #41
2 (1.9m)	Uncoded areas are camel #43 Continental Stitches

Color numbers given are for Uniek Needloft plastic canvas yarn.

Cut out

Mug of Root Beer
23 holes x 25 holes
Cut 1

Shirley Temple

Illustration on page 170

COLOR KEY
Shirley Temple
Yards	Plastic Canvas Yarn
4 (3.7m)	▨ Watermelon #55
	╱ Attach drink umbrella
	╲ Attach toothpick with cherry glued on (see pattern)

Color number given is for Uniek Needloft plastic canvas yarn.

Shirley Temple
19 holes x 16 holes
Cut 1

Margarita

COLOR KEY
Margarita
Yards	Plastic Canvas Yarn
2 (1.9m)	▨ Moss #25
2 (1.9m)	☐ White #41
	⬇⬇ Attach salt (stuffing pellets)

Color numbers given are for Uniek Needloft plastic canvas yarn.

Margarita
20 holes x 25 holes
Cut 1

This & That

From sports to southwest decor, this chapter of motifs has something for everyone.

Crescent Moon

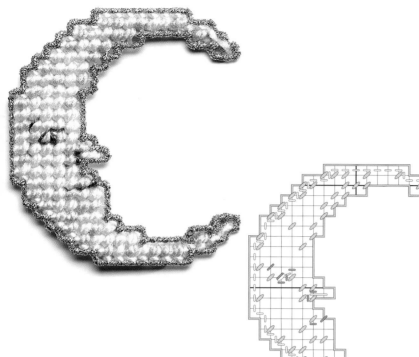

COLOR KEY
Crescent Moon

Yards	Plastic Canvas Yarn
1 (1m)	☐ Beige #40
1 (1m)	☐ White #41
2 (1.9m)	Uncoded areas are eggshell #39 Continental Stitches
	⟋ Eggshell #39 Straight Stitch
	⟋ White #41 (2-ply) Backstitch
	⟋ White #41 (1-ply) Straight Stitch
2 (1.9m)	**¹⁄₈-Inch/0.3cm Ribbon**
	☐ Gold #002HL
1 (1m)	**#5 Pearl Cotton**
	⟋ Ultra dark beaver gray #844 Backstitch and Straight Stitch

Color numbers given are for Uniek Needloft plastic canvas yarn, Kreinik ¹⁄₈-inch Ribbon and DMC #5 pearl cotton.

Crescent Moon
19 holes x 22 holes
Cut 1

Honey Beehive

COLOR KEY
Honey Beehive

Yards	Plastic Canvas Yarn
4 (3.7m)	☐ Beige #40
2 (1.9m)	Uncoded areas are baby yellow #21 Continental Stitches
1 (1m)	⟋ White Backstitch
	#5 Pearl Cotton
1 (1m)	■ Ultra dark coffee brown #938
2 (1.9m)	⟋ Very dark beige gray #640 Straight Stitch
	⟋ Ultra dark coffee brown #938 Backstitch and Straight Stitch

Color numbers given are for Uniek Needloft plastic canvas yarn and DMC #5 pearl cotton.

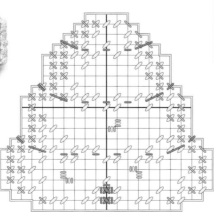

Honey Beehive
20 holes x 19 holes
Cut 1

Mushroom

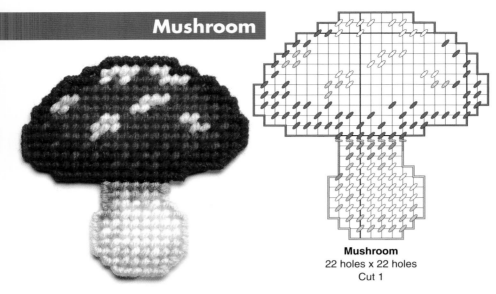

Mushroom
22 holes x 22 holes
Cut 1

COLOR KEY
Mushroom

Yards	Worsted Weight Yarn
1 (1m)	☐ Eggshell #111
1 (1m)	☐ Tan #334
1 (1m)	☐ Warm brown #336
2 (1.9m)	■ Cardinal #917
2 (1.9m)	Uncoded areas are country red #914 Continental Stitches

#5 Pearl Cotton

Yards	
1 (1m)	∕ Ultra dark coffee brown #938 Backstitch

Color numbers given are for Coats & Clark Red Heart Classic worsted weight yarn Art. E267 and DMC #5 pearl cotton.

Beehive

COLOR KEY
Beehive

Yards	Worsted Weight Yarn
4 (3.7m)	☐ Gold
1 (1m)	☐ Denim heather
1 (1m)	☐ Dark yellow green
	∕ Dark yellow green Backstitch
	● Attach 1-inch/2.5cm black button with dark yellow green

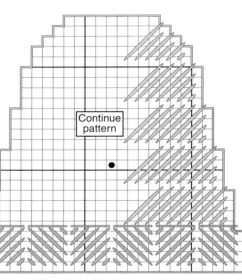

Continue pattern

Beehive
25 holes x 25 holes
Cut 1

Cactus

COLOR KEY
Cactus

Yards	Plastic Canvas Yarn
5 (4.6m)	☐ Fern #23
	○ Attach 14mm translucent rose flower bead
	● Attach 4mm opaque green bead

Color number given is for Uniek Needloft plastic canvas yarn.

Cactus
16 holes x 25 holes
Cut 1

Country Lantern

Illustration on page 170

COLOR KEY
Country Lantern

Yards	Plastic Canvas Yarn
5 (4.6m)	■ Christmas red #02
1 (1m)	☐ White #41
1 (1m)	☐ Yellow #57
	┃ Attach flame (see pattern)
	● Attach ½-inch/1.3cm red dome button
	⤙ Attach handle (18-gauge red craft wire)

Color numbers given are for Uniek Needloft plastic canvas yarn.

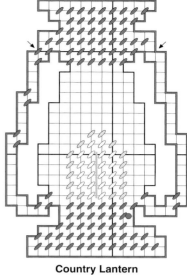

Country Lantern
17 holes x 25 holes
Cut 1

Country Heart

COLOR KEY
Country Heart

Yards	Worsted Weight Yarn
3 (2.8m)	☐ Gold
2 (1.9m)	☐ Off-white
2 (1.9m)	☐ Denim heather
2 (1.9m)	■ Windsor blue
2 (1.9m)	☐ Purple
2 (1.9m)	╱ Black Backstitch and Overcasting
	● Attach ¾-inch/1.9cm off-white button with off-white

Country Heart
25 holes x 25 holes
Cut 1

Basket of Fruit

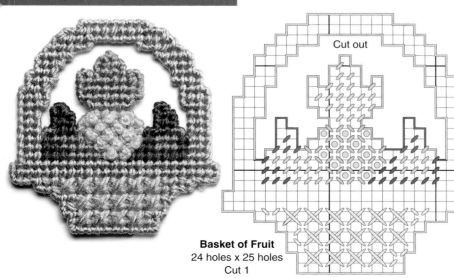

Cut out

Basket of Fruit
24 holes x 25 holes
Cut 1

COLOR KEY
Basket of Fruit

Yards	Plastic Canvas Yarn
1 (1m)	■ Burgundy #03
1 (1m)	☐ Tangerine #11
1 (1m)	☐ Fern #23
1 (1m)	■ Holly #27
6 (5.5m)	☐ Sail blue #35
1 (1m)	☐ Watermelon #55
	Uncoded areas are sail blue #35 Continental Stitches
1 (1m)	○ Yellow #57 French Knot

Color numbers given are for Uniek Needloft plastic canvas yarn.

Acorn

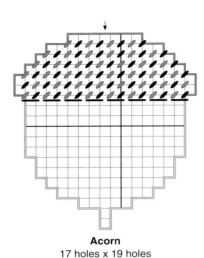

COLOR KEY
Acorn

Yards	Plastic Canvas Yarn
1 (1m)	■ Black #00
1 (1m)	▨ Cinnamon #14
3 (2.8m)	Uncoded area is camel #43 Continental Stitches
╱	Camel #43 Overcasting
╱	Black #00 Backstitch
↓	Attach 1³⁄₈-inch/ 3.5cm-long twig

Color numbers given are for Uniek Needloft plastic canvas yarn.

Acorn
17 holes x 19 holes
Cut 1

Bubble Bath

Bubble Bath
18 holes x 16 holes
Cut 1

COLOR KEY
Bubble Bath

Yards	Plastic Canvas Yarn
1 (1m)	▢ Silver #37
1 (1m)	▢ Gray #38
2 (1.9m)	Uncoded areas are white #41 Continental Stitches
╱	White #41 Overcasting
▢	Attach bubbles (assorted sizes white pearl beads)

Color numbers given are for Uniek Needloft plastic canvas yarn.

Thatched Cottage

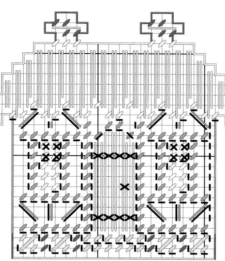

Thatched Cottage
23 holes x 24 holes
Cut 1

COLOR KEY
Thatched Cottage

Yards	Plastic Canvas Yarn
3 (2.8m)	■ Cinnamon #14
1 (1m)	☐ Baby blue #36
1 (1m)	☐ Silver #37
1 (1m)	■ Gray #38
1 (1m)	☐ White #41
2 (1.9)	Uncoded areas are eggshell #39 Continental Stitches
1 (1m)	⁄ Moss #25 Overcasting
	⁄ Cinnamon #14 Straight Stitch
	⁄ Silver #37 Straight Stitch
2 (1.9m)	⁄ Beige #40 Straight Stitch
3 (2.8m)	⁄ Camel #43 Straight Stitch and Overcasting
	#5 Pearl Cotton
4 (3.7m)	✓ Black Backstitch and Straight Stitch

Color numbers given are for Uniek Needloft plastic canvas yarn.

Tree

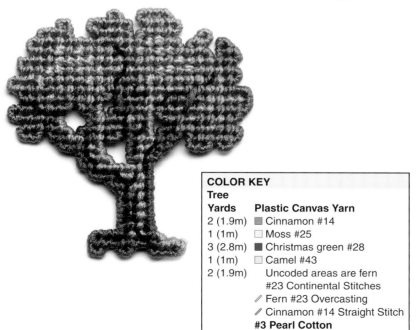

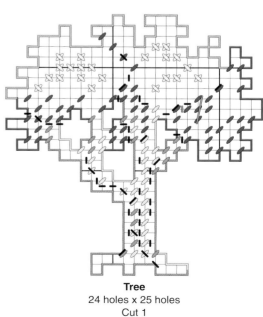

Tree
24 holes x 25 holes
Cut 1

COLOR KEY
Tree

Yards	Plastic Canvas Yarn
2 (1.9m)	■ Cinnamon #14
1 (1m)	☐ Moss #25
3 (2.8m)	■ Christmas green #28
1 (1m)	☐ Camel #43
2 (1.9m)	Uncoded areas are fern #23 Continental Stitches
	⁄ Fern #23 Overcasting
	⁄ Cinnamon #14 Straight Stitch
	#3 Pearl Cotton
1 (1m)	✓ Black Backstitch and Straight Stitch

Color numbers given are for Uniek Needloft plastic canvas yarn.

Spool-o'-Thread

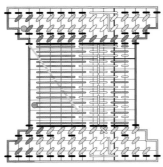

Spool-o'-Thread
14 holes x 15 holes
Cut 1

Get Well Soon

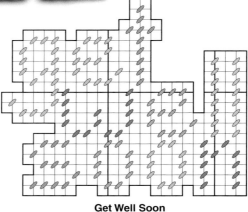

Get Well Soon
23 holes x 19 holes
Cut 1 from
yellow plastic canvas

Watering Can

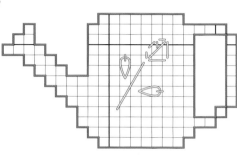

Watering Can
22 holes x 13 holes
Cut 1

Garden Trowel

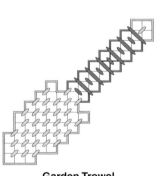

Garden Trowel
14 holes x 14 holes
Cut 1

Garden Hand Rake

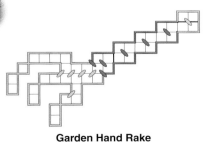

Garden Hand Rake
18 holes x 11 holes
Cut 1

Abstract Star

Abstract Star
25 holes x 25 holes
Cut 1
Fill in points of star
following point diagram

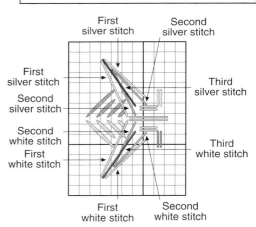

First silver stitch

Second silver stitch

First silver stitch

Third silver stitch

Second silver stitch

Second white stitch

First white stitch

Third white stitch

First white stitch

Second white stitch

Abstract Star Point Diagram

Abstract Cube

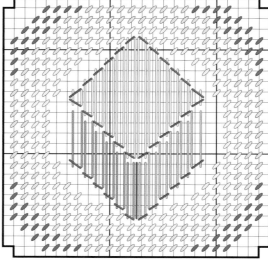

Abstract Cube
25 holes x 25 holes
Cut 1

Abstract Sphere

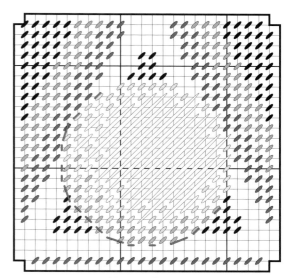

Abstract Sphere
25 holes x 25 holes
Cut 1

COLOR KEY
Abstract Sphere

Yards	Worsted Weight Yarn
2 (1.9m)	☐ White #1
3 (2.8m)	■ Black #12
2 (1.9m)	■ Coffee #365
1 (1m)	■ Nickel #401
1 (1m)	☐ Silver #412
2 (1.9m)	■ Cardinal #917
2 (1.9m)	Uncoded areas are cherry red #912 Continental Stitches
#3 Pearl Cotton	
1 (1m)	╱ Black Backstitch and Straight Stitch

Color numbers given are for Coats & Clark Red Heart Classic worsted weight yarn Art. E267.

School Stuff

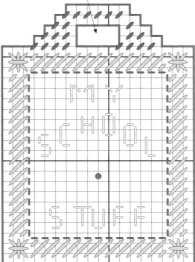

School Stuff
18 holes x 25 holes
Cut 1

COLOR KEY
School Stuff

Yards	Plastic Canvas Yarn
2 (1.9m)	■ Red #01
2 (1.9m)	☐ Sandstone #16
4 (3.7m)	Uncoded background is black #00 Continental Stitches
	╱ Red #02 (2-ply) Backstitch
1 (1m)	╱ White #41 (1-ply) Backstitch
	● Attach apple button
	↘ Thread 18 inches/45.7cm (5/8-inch/1.6cm-wide) Measure Up ribbon and tie in a bow

Color numbers given are for Uniek Needloft plastic canvas yarn; ribbon from Offray.

Patriotic Quilt Block

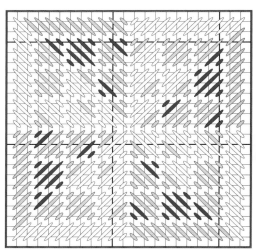

Patriotic Quilt Block
23 holes x 23 holes
Cut 1

COLOR KEY
Patriotic Quilt Block

Yards	Plastic Canvas Yarn
3 (2.8m)	■ Burgundy #03
1 (1m)	■ Cinnamon #14
3 (2.8m)	☐ Gold #17
2 (1.9m)	☐ Eggshell #39
2 (1.9m)	■ Dark royal #48

Color numbers given are for Uniek Needloft plastic canvas yarn.

Winter Quilt Block

COLOR KEY
Winter Quilt Block

Yards	Plastic Canvas Yarn
2 (1.9m)	☐ Royal #32
3 (2.8m)	☐ Silver #37
3 (2.8m)	☐ White #41
3 (2.8m)	■ Dark royal #48

Color numbers given are for Uniek Needloft plastic canvas yarn.

Winter Quilt Block
23 holes x 23 holes
Cut 1

Spring Quilt Block

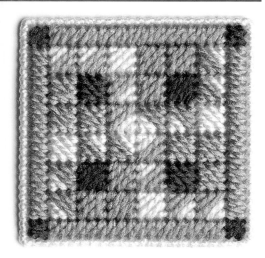

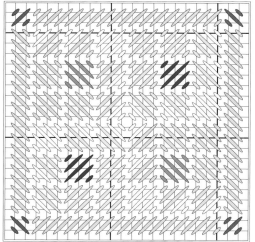

COLOR KEY
Spring Quilt Block

Yards	Plastic Canvas Yarn
3 (2.8m)	☐ Moss #25
1 (1m)	■ Forest #29
2 (1.9m)	☐ Sail blue #35
3 (2.8m)	☐ White #41
2 (1.9m)	☐ Lilac #45
1 (1m)	■ Purple #46
1 (1m)	■ Dark royal #48

Color numbers given are for Uniek Needloft plastic canvas yarn.

Spring Quilt Block
23 holes x 23 holes
Cut 1

Summer Quilt Block

Summer Quilt Block
23 holes x 23 holes
Cut 1

Autumn Quilt Block

Autumn Quilt Block
23 holes x 23 holes
Cut 1

Igloo

Illustrations on page 170

COLOR KEY
Igloo
Yards	Plastic Canvas Yarn
1 (1m)	■ Black #00
7 (6.5m)	Uncoded background is white #41 Continental Stitches
	⁄ White #41 Overcasting
	6-Strand Embroidery Floss
3 (2.8m)	⁄ Black (3-ply) Backstitch and Straight Stitch
	↓ Attach smoke (see pattern)
	● Attach flames (see pattern)
	– Attach firewood (see pattern)

Color numbers given are for Uniek Needloft plastic canvas yarn.

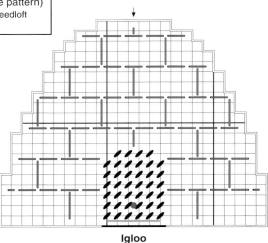

Igloo
25 holes x 20 holes
Cut 1

Eskimo

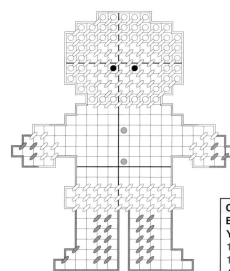

Eskimo
21 holes x 25 holes
Cut 1

COLOR KEY
Eskimo
Yards	Plastic Canvas Yarn
1 (1m)	☐ Pink #07
1 (1m)	▨ Cinnamon #14
4 (3.7m)	☐ White #41
2 (1.9m)	Uncoded areas are camel #43 Continental Stitches
	⁄ Camel #43 Overcasting
	○ White #41 loops (¹⁄₄ to ³⁄₄ inch/0.6 to 1.9cm long)
	6-Strand Embroidery Floss
1 (1m)	● Black (2-ply) French Knot
	○ Attach ³⁄₁₆-inch/0.5cm white button

Color numbers given are for Uniek Needloft plastic canvas yarn.

Black, White & Gray Pottery

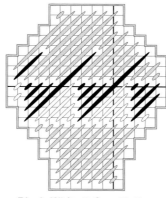

Black, White & Gray Pottery
15 holes x 18 holes
Cut 1

COLOR KEY
Black, White & Gray Pottery

Yards	Plastic Canvas Yarn
1 (1m)	■ Black #00
3 (2.8m)	▨ Gray #38
1 (1m)	☐ White #41

Color numbers given are for Uniek Needloft plastic canvas yarn.

Earth-Tones Pottery

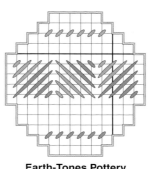

Earth-Tones Pottery
13 holes x 14 holes
Cut 1

COLOR KEY
Earth-Tones Pottery

Yards	Worsted Weight Yarn
2 (1.9m)	Uncoded areas are buff #334 Continental Stitches
	∕ Buff #334 Overcasting
	Plastic Canvas Yarn
1 (1m)	▨ Sundown #10
1 (1m)	▨ Brown #15

Color numbers given are for Coats & Clark Red Heart Super Saver worsted weight yarn Art. E300 and Uniek Needloft plastic canvas yarn.

Southwestern Pot

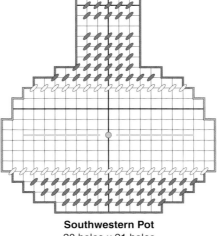

Southwestern Pot
20 holes x 21 holes
Cut 1

COLOR KEY
Southwestern Pot

Yards	Plastic Canvas Yarn
3 (2.8m)	▨ Brown #15
1 (1m)	☐ Eggshell #39
3 (2.8m)	Uncoded areas are rust #09 Continental Stitches
	∕ Rust #09 Overcasting
	● Attach 12mm round turquoise cabochon
	— Attach feather

Color numbers given are for Uniek Needloft plastic canvas yarn.

Musical Notes Quarter Note
8 holes x 17 holes
Cut 1

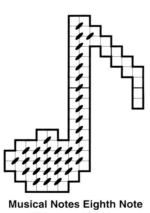

Musical Notes Eighth Note
13 holes x 17 holes
Cut 1

COLOR KEY
Musical Notes
Yards	Metallic Cord
8 (7.4m)	■ Multi black #109

Color number given is for Darice metallic cord.

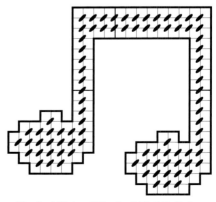

Musical Notes Attached Eighth Notes
19 holes x 18 holes
Cut 1

Heart Coaster

COLOR KEY
Heart Coaster

Yards	Worsted Weight Yarn
4 (3.7m)	☐ Off-white
3 (2.8m)	▨ Denim heather
2 (1.9m)	▨ Gold
2 (1.9m)	Uncoded background is claret Continental Stitches
2 (1.9m)	⁄ Light brown Backstitch and Overcasting
	○ Attach ³/₈-inch/1cm denim button with gold

#3 Pearl Cotton

2 (1.9m)	⁄ Black Backstitch and Straight Stitch

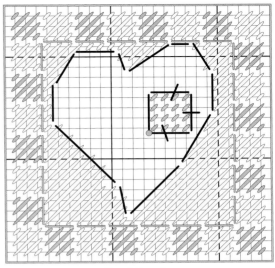

Heart Coaster
25 holes x 25 holes
Cut 1

Birdhouse Coaster

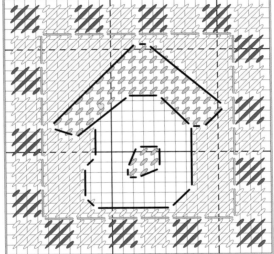

COLOR KEY
Birdhouse Coaster

Yards	Worsted Weight Yarn
4 (3.7m)	☐ Off-white
3 (2.8m)	■ Claret
2 (1.9m)	▨ Denim heather
2 (1.9)	Uncoded background is gold Continental Stitches
2 (1.9)	⁄ Light brown Backstitch and Overcasting
	♡ Attach ⁷/₁₆-inch/1.1cm white heart button with claret

#3 Pearl Cotton

2 (1.9m)	⁄ Black Backstitch and Straight Stitch

Birdhouse Coaster
25 holes x 25 holes
Cut 1

Sunflower Coaster

COLOR KEY
Sunflower Coaster

Yards	Worsted Weight Yarn
4 (3.7m)	☐ Off-white
4 (3.7m)	■ Claret
2 (1.9m)	▨ Light brown
1 (1m)	▨ Denim heather
2 (1.9)	Uncoded background is gold Continental Stitches
	⁄ Light brown Backstitch
	○ Attach ³/₈-inch/1cm light brown button with off-white

#3 Pearl Cotton

2 (1.9m)	⁄ Black Backstitch and Straight Stitch

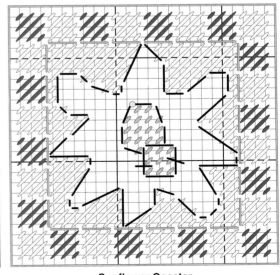

Sunflower Coaster
25 holes x 25 holes
Cut 1

White-Winged Bee

Continued from page 11

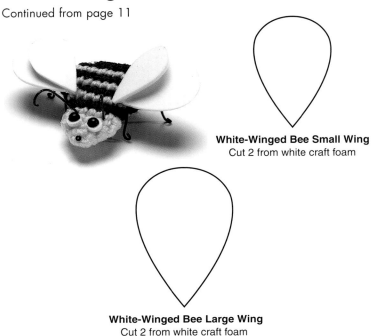

White-Winged Bee Small Wing
Cut 2 from white craft foam

White-Winged Bee Large Wing
Cut 2 from white craft foam

Snow-White Dove

Continued from page 12

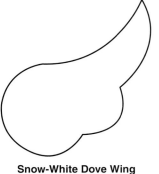

Snow-White Dove Wing
Cut 2 from white craft foam

Rooster in Flight

Continued from page 12

Rooster in Flight Foot
Cut 2 from black craft foam

Mr. Gobbler

Continued from page 13

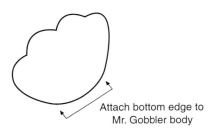

Attach bottom edge to
Mr. Gobbler body

Mr. Gobbler Brown Wing
Cut 1 from brown craft foam

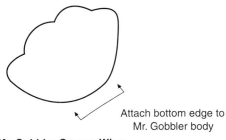

Attach bottom edge to
Mr. Gobbler body

Mr. Gobbler Orange Wing
Cut 1 from orange craft foam

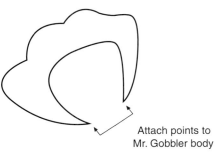

Attach points to
Mr. Gobbler body

Mr. Gobbler Yellow Wing
Cut 1 from yellow craft foam

Long-Tailed Rooster

Continued from page 15

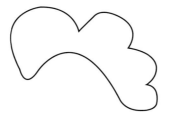

Long-Tailed Rooster Comb
Cut 1 from red craft foam

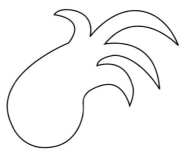

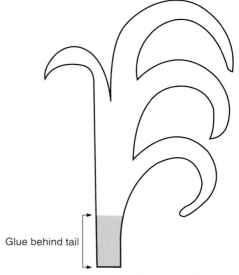

Glue behind tail

Long-Tailed Rooster Top Beak
Cut 1 from yellow craft foam

Long-Tailed Rooster Wing
Cut 1 from white craft foam

Long-Tailed Rooster Tail
Cut 1 from white craft foam

Wide-Eyed Duck

Continued from page 17

Attach to duck body

Wide-Eyed Duck Wing
Cut 1 from white craft foam

Hungry Bunny

Continued from page 21

Hungry Bunny Large Ear
Cut 2 from camel felt

Hungry Bunny Small Ear
Cut 2 from white felt

Spot

Continued from page 18

Attach tip to head

Spot Ear
Cut 2 from black felt
or faux suede

Wise Old Owl

Continued from page 20

Wise Old Owl Foot
Cut 2 from black craft foam

Leopold

Continued from page 21

Portly Pig

Continued from page 22

Portly Pig Tail Tip
Cut 2 from light peach felt
Glue together over tip of tail

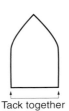

Tack together

Portly Pig Ear
Cut 1 from light peach felt

Leopold Nose
Cut 1 from black faux suede

Baby With Bottle

Continued from page 52

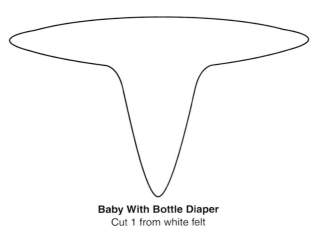

Baby With Bottle Diaper
Cut 1 from white felt

Western Vest

Continued from page 65

Cut fringe along
dotted lines
Western Vest Pocket Flap
Cut 2 from beige brown
felt or faux suede

Cut fringe along
dotted lines
Western Vest Bolo Tie
Cut 1 from beige brown
felt or faux suede

Camel Cowboy Boot

Continued from page 65

Cut fringe along
dotted lines

Camel Cowboy Boot Fringe
Cut 1 from beige brown
felt or faux suede

Bulldozer

Continued from page 67

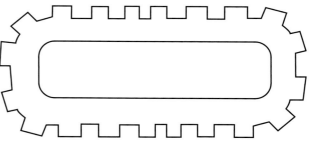

Bulldozer Traction Tire
Cut 1 from
black craft foam

Girls, Girls, Girls

Ballet Slippers

Continued from page 76

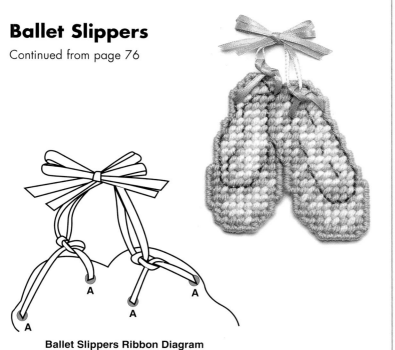

Ballet Slippers Ribbon Diagram
For each slipper, bring ends of one
ribbon length up at points A.
Tie each length in a knot, then
bring both lengths together
and tie in a double bow.

Glove Heart

Continued from page 85

Glove Heart
Cut 2 each from lightweight
cardboard and off-white rayon,
reversing 1 before cutting
Glue rayon to cardboard

Snowman

Continued from page 96

Snowman Mitten
Cut 4 from red
faux suede or felt

Snowman Hat Brim
Cut 1 from black
faux suede or felt
Slip over hat

Red Flower Heart

Continued from page 98

Red Flower Heart Leaves
Cut 2 large leaves
from green craft foam
Cut 1 small leaf
from green craft foam

Welcoming Santa

Continued from page 117

Welcoming Santa Mustache
Cut 1 from white craft foam

Waving Santa

Continued from page 118

Glue to Santa's face

Waving Santa Beard
Cut 1 from
white plush felt

Waving Santa Mustache
Cut 1 from
white plush felt

Attach white pompom

Waving Santa Hat
Cut 1 from red craft foam

Pink Flamingo

Continued from page 135

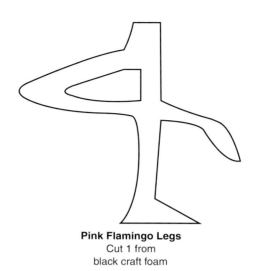

Pink Flamingo Legs
Cut 1 from
black craft foam

Hamburger

Continued from page 143

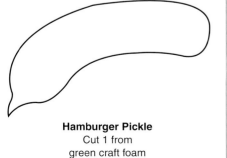

Hamburger Pickle
Cut 1 from
green craft foam

Pear

Continued from page 144

Pear Leaf
Cut 1 from
green craft foam;
add leaf veins with
black fine-point marker

Strawberry

Continued from page 144

Strawberry Stem
Cut 1 from
light green craft foam;
attach to strawberry top

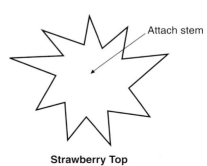

Attach stem

Strawberry Top
Cut 1 from
light green craft foam

Pineapple
Continued from page 145

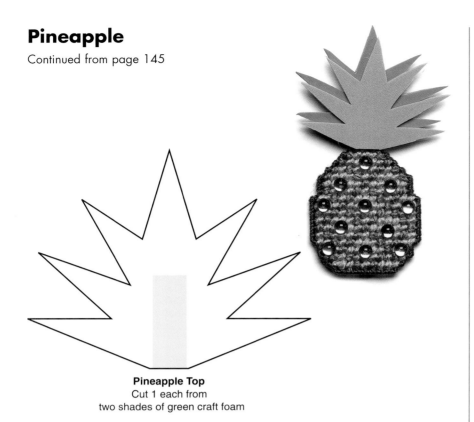

Pineapple Top
Cut 1 each from
two shades of green craft foam

Shirley Temple
Continued from page 147

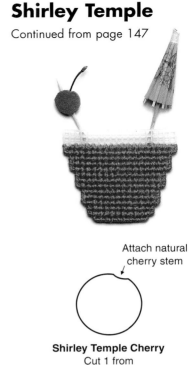

Attach natural
cherry stem

Shirley Temple Cherry
Cut 1 from
red craft foam;
brush with tacky glue

This & That

Country Lantern
Continued from page 151

Country Lantern Flame
Cut 1 from
orange craft foam

Igloo
Continued from page 160

Igloo Firewood
Cut 1 from
brown craft foam

Igloo Large Flame
Cut 1 from
yellow craft foam

Igloo Small Flame
Cut 1 from
red craft foam

Igloo Smoke
Cut 1 from
white craft foam

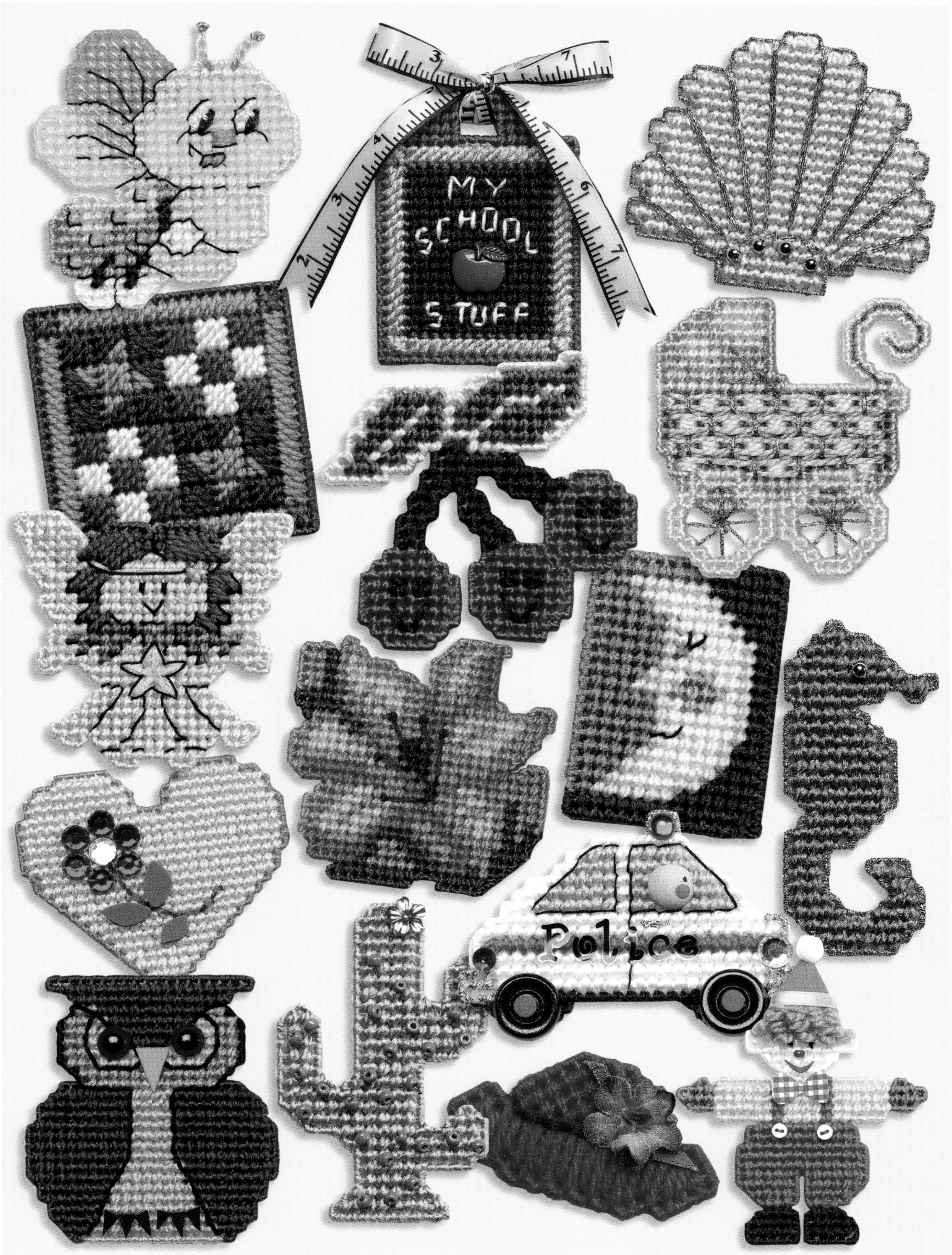
MY
SCHOOL
STUFF
Police

Special Thanks

We would like to acknowledge and thank the following designers whose original work has been published in this collection. We appreciate and value their creativity and dedication to designing quality plastic canvas projects!

Angie Arickx

Holidays: Blue & Silver Cross, Green & Gold Cross, Pink & Gold Cross, Purple & Pearl Cross
Minis: Blue Quilt Block, Green Quilt Block, Pink Quilt Block, Purple Quilt Block
This & That: Autumn Quilt Block, Patriotic Quilt Block, Spring Quilt Block, Summer Quilt Block, Winter Quilt Block

Ronda Bryce

Babies: Baby Boy Star, Baby Girl Star, Man in the Moon, Teddy Bear Black, Yellow Star
Boys' Toys: Hammer, Pliers, Screwdriver
By the Sea: Anchor
Critters: Duck, Hummingbird, Yellow Duck
Florals: Framed Rose
Girls, Girls, Girls: Framed Purse, Unicorn
Holidays: Framed Cross
Minis: Alpha Omega, Chi Rho, IHS, Palm Branch, Quilt Basket, Quilt Bow, Quilt Heart, Quilt Star, The Sign of the Fish

Pam Bull

Boys' Toys: Red & Blue Crayons
By the Sea: Sailboat
Munchies: Apple, Deep-Dish Pie
This & That: Birdhouse Coaster, Beehive, Country Heart, Heart Coaster, Sunflower Coaster

Mary T. Cosgrove

Holidays: Happy New Year Ball, Happy New Year Banner, Happy New Year Hat & Mask, Happy New Year Horn & Notes
Munchies: Asparagus, Banana, Cauliflower, Cherries, Chili Pepper, Pea Pod

Carol Dace

Girls, Girls, Girls: Large Red Hat, Small Red Hat

Holidays: Irishman, Jingle Bell Reindeer, Let It Snow Snowman, Lovey Snowman, Mrs. Claus, Santa Claus, Snowman With Blue Scarf, Uncle Sam

Janelle Giese

Babies: Binky Bunny, Decorative Rattle, Embroidered Bootee, Golden Buggy, Hot Air Balloon, Mini Birth Sampler, Tubby Duck, Rocking Horse
Boys' Toys: Train Engine
By the Sea: Antique Glass Float, Basket Cockle, Bay Lighthouse, Bouncing Beach Ball, Colorful Kite, Dolphin, Fantasy Fish, Frilled Dogwinkle, Lighthouse, Pink Scallop, Rough Keyhole Limpet, Royal Sand Castle, Sand Dollar, Seagull, Thomas Point Shoal Lighthouse, Whale, Wind Sock
Critters: Cottontail, Fantasy Bird, Fantasy Bug, Puffy Bunny, Puffy Kitty, Puffy Puppy, Raccoon, Rubber Ducky, Vintage Butterfly
Florals: Cabbage Rose, Dandelion, Pansy Nosegay, Tulip Circle
Girls, Girls, Girls: Affection Fairy, Ballet Slippers, Balloon Bear, Bunnymobile, Dollhouse, Dreams Fairy, Glowing Star, Jeweled Tiara, Satin Bow, Satin Doll, Wishes Fairy
Holidays: Ghostly Night
Munchies: Chocolate Chip Cookie
This & That: Abstract Cube, Abstract Sphere, Abstract Star, Crescent Moon, Honey Beehive, Mushroom, Spool-o'-Thread, Thatched Cottage, Tree

Kathleen Hurley

Babies: Hobby Horse, Stuffed Teddy Bear
Boys' Toys: Cheerful Clown, Jack-in-the-Box
Critters: Bluebird, Bunny & Blossoms, Chickadee, Decorated Ducky, Hummingbird & Flower, Perky Penguin, Plump Penguin, Spring Chicken

Florals: Basket of Pansies, Blue Iris, Morning Glory, Purple Pansy, Rose Blush, Spring Posies, Strawberry Blossoms, Tiger Lily, Watering Can Blossoms
Girls, Girls, Girls: Maiden With Bouquet
Holidays: Blushing Snowman, Bunny With Egg, Candy Cane, Christmas Angel, Christmas Bell, Christmas Bows, Christmas Horn, Decorated Egg, Dressed-up Bunny, Holly Leaf, Jolly Snowman, Jolly St. Nick, Lamppost Noel, Peek-a-Boo Bunny, Peek-a-Boo Pumpkin, Santa Face, Side-View Santa, Spooky Characters
Munchies: Crisp Apple, Crunchy Carrots, Juicy Pear, Red Beet
This & That: Basket of Fruit

Judi Kauffman

Minis: Red, White & Blue Square 1; Red, White & Blue Square 2; Red, White & Blue Square 3

Susan Leinberger

Girls, Girls, Girls: Black Ankle Strap Shoe, Casual Checked Mule, Feminine Finery Hanger, Feminine Finery Purse, Feminine Finery Red Hat, Feminine Finery Red Shoe, Flowered Spike Heel, Glass Slipper, Pink Polka-Dot Sling Back, Blue Willow Creamer, Blue Willow Saucer, Blue Willow Sugar Bowl, Blue Willow Teacup, Blue Willow Teapot
This & That: School Stuff

Lee Lindeman

Babies: Baby in the Bathtub, Baby With Bottle, Blue Baby Buggy
Boys' Toys: Blue Pickup Truck, Bulldozer, Clarence the Clown, Country Guitar, Camel Cowboy Boot, Cowboy Hat, Dump Truck, Fire Engine, Fire Hydrant, Fireman's Hat, Go Sign, Ice-Cream Truck, Moon Man, Police Car, Red Boat, Red Car, School Bus, Sport Shirt, Stop Sign, Taxi, Traffic Light, Western Vest, Work Boot
By the Sea: Green Fish, Pink Flamingo, Sea Horse, Seashell, Starfish
Critters: Big Bee, Black Cat, Black Spider, Blue-Eyed Bunny, Bouncing Bunny, Chipper, Garden Worm, Giant Ladybug, Gray Squirrel, Hungry Bunny, Leopold,

Long-Tailed Rooster, Mansfield the Mouse, Mr. Gobbler, Mr. Penguin, Playful Bear, Portly Pig, Rooster in Flight, Silly Turtle, Sitting Bunny, Smiling Frog, Snow-White Dove, Spot, Tiny Tiger, White-Winged Bee, Wide-Eyed Duck, Wise Old Owl

Girls, Girls, Girls: Baby-Blue Bow Heart, Baby-Blue Heart, Bunny in Blue Jumper, Dancing Frog, Lollipop, Glove Heart, Red Bow, Ribbon-Trimmed Heart Frame

Holidays: Bat, Blue Angel, Blue Mitten, Egg 1, Egg 2, Egg 3, Egg 4, Figure Skate, Ghost, Gold Bead Ornament, Gold Star Ornament, Mirror Heart, Pink Roses Ornament, Red Bead Ornament, Red Flower Heart, Red Rhinestone Ornament, Red Santa Hat, Santa in the Chimney, Smiling Pumpkin, Snowman, Spring Egg 1, Spring Egg 2, Spring Egg 3, Spring Egg 4, Striped Heart, Waving Santa, Welcoming Santa, Witch

Minis: Southwest Square 1, Southwest Square 2, Southwest Square 3

Munchies: Carrot, Cupcake, Gold-Rimmed Teacup, Hamburger, Ice-Cream Bar, Ice-Cream Cone, Ice-Cream Sundae, Margarita, Mug of Root Beer, Pear, Pineapple, Shirley Temple, Strawberry

This & That: Acorn, Cactus, Country Lantern, Eskimo, Igloo, Southwestern Pot

Alida Macor

Babies: Mini Clown

Boys' Toys: Mini Train Caboose, Mini Train Coal Car, Mini Train Locomotive, Mini Train Passenger Car

Critters: Ornery Kitty

Holidays: Mini Christmas Tree

Terry Ricioli

Babies: Blue-Capped Baby Bottle, Golden Teddy, Pink Baby Carriage, Shining Star, Smiley, Sunshine, Yellow Rattle

Boys' Toys: Kite

By the Sea: Crab, Flip-Flop Sandal, Lobster, Orange Fish

Critters: Bitty Bunny, Ducky, Little Ladybug, Lovebird, Plaid Butterfly, Pocket-Pal Frog, Pretty Pony, Yellow Butterfly

Florals: Bright Flower, Daffodil, Iris, Pink Tulip, Rosebud

Girls, Girls, Girls: Ballerina; Cheerleader; Fairy Godmother; Hat, Purse & High Heel Show

Holidays: Gingerbread Boy, Gingerbread Girl, Golden Cross, Heart & Stripes Forever, Mortarboard, Pastel Easter Egg, Patriotic Heart, Pint-Size Evergreen, Pint-Size Snowman, Valentine Kiss

Minis: Amish Square, Log Cabin, Log Cabin Variation, Nine Patch, Southwestern Design

Munchies: Delicate Teacup & Saucer, Flowered Teapot

This & That: Garden Hand Rake, Garden Trowel, Get Well Soon, Watering Can

Ruby Thacker

Babies: Duck Pull Toy, White-Capped Baby Bottle

Boys' Toys: Baseball & Bat, Brown Cowboy Boots, Cow Skull, Little Red Wagon, Pink & Purple Kite, Primary Colors Kite

By the Sea: Colorful Beach Ball, Sand Bucket & Shovel, Sand Castle

Holidays: Angel With Charm, Blue Easter Egg, Jester's Hat, Masquerade Half-Mask, Masquerade Mask, One-Star Firecracker, Pink Easter Egg, Reindeer, Striped Firecracker, Three-Star Firecracker

Munchies: Chocolate Milk Shake, Double-Dip Sundae, Harvest Corn, Strawberry Ice-Cream Cone, Summer Corn

This & That: Black, White & Gray Pottery; Bubble Bath; Earth-Tones Pottery; Musical Notes

Kathy Wirth

Critters: Peeking Cat

Florals: Bicolored Floral

Holidays: Patriotic Star

Buyer's Guide

When looking for a specific material, first check your local craft and retail stores. If you're unable to locate a product locally, contact the manufacturers listed below for the closest retail source in your area or a mail-order source.

Coats & Clark Inc.
Consumer Service
P.O. Box 12229
Greenville, SC 29612-0229
(800) 648-1479
www.coatsandclark.com

DMC Corp.
Hackensack Ave., Bldg. 10A
South Kearny, NJ 07032-4688
(800) 275-4117
www.dmc-usa.com

Gay Bowles Sales Inc.
P.O. Box 1060
Janesville, WI 53547
(800) 447-1332
www.millhill.com

Kreinik Mfg. Co. Inc.
3106 Lord Baltimore Drive #101
Baltimore, MD 21244-2871
(800) 537-2166
www.kreinik.com

Lion Brand Yarn Co.
34 W. 15th St.
New York, NY 10011
(800) 258-9276
www.lionbrand.com

Rainbow Gallery
7412 Fulton Ave., #5
North Hollywood, CA 91605
(818) 982-4496
www.rainbowgallery.com

Uniek
Mail-order source:
Annie's Attic
1 Annie Ln.
Big Sandy, TX 75755
(800) 582-6643
www.anniesattic.com

Stitch Guide

Use the following diagrams to expand your plastic canvas stitching skills. For each diagram, bring needle up through canvas at the red number one and go back down through the canvas at the red number two. The second stitch is numbered in green. Always bring needle up through the canvas at odd numbers and take it back down through the canvas at the even numbers.

Background Stitches

The following stitches are used for filling in large areas of canvas. The Continental Stitch is the most commonly used stitch. Other stitches, such as the Condensed Mosaic and Scotch Stitch, fill in large areas of canvas more quickly than the Continental Stitch because their stitches cover a larger area of canvas.

Continental Stitch

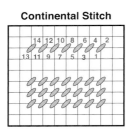

Condensed Mosaic

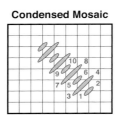

Alternating Continental

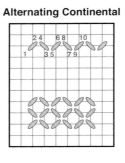

Cross Stitch

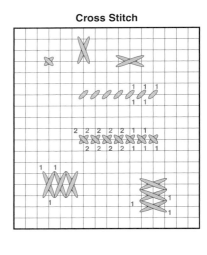

Long Stitch

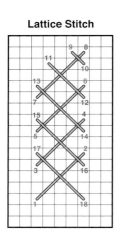

Scotch Stitch

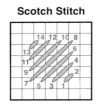

Slanting Gobelin

Embroidery Stitches

These stitches are worked on top of a stitched area to add detail to the project. Embroidery stitches are usually worked with one strand of yarn, several strands of pearl cotton or several strands of embroidery floss.

Lattice Stitch

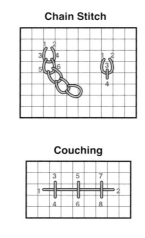

Chain Stitch

Couching

Straight Stitch

Running Stitch

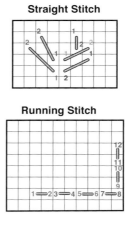

Fly Stitch

Backstitch

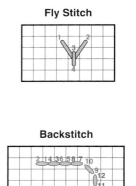

Embroidery Stitches

French Knot

Bring needle up through canvas. Wrap yarn around needle 1 to 3 times, depending on desired size of knot; take needle back through canvas through same hole.

Lazy Daisy

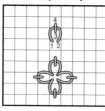

Bring yarn needle up through canvas, then back down in same hole, leaving a small loop. Then, bring needle up inside loop; take needle back down through canvas on other side of loop.

Loop Stitch/Turkey Loop Stitch

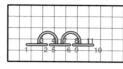

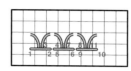

The top diagram shows this stitch left intact. This is an effective stitch for giving a project dimensional hair. The bottom diagram demonstrates the cut loop stitch. Because each stitch is anchored, cutting it will not cause the stitches to come out. A group of cut loop stitches gives a fluffy, soft look and feel to your project.

Specialty Stitches

The following stitches can be worked either on top of a previously stitched area or directly onto the canvas. Like the embroidery stitches, these too add wonderful detail and give your stitching additional interest and texture.

Satin Stitches

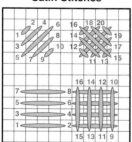

Smyrna Cross

Finishing Stitches

Overcast/Whipstitch

Overcasting and Whipstitching are used to finish the outer edges of the canvas. Overcasting is done to finish one edge at a time. Whipstitching is used to stitch two or more pieces of canvas together along an edge. For both Overcasting and Whipstitching, work one stitch in each hole along straight edges and inside corners, and two or three stitches in outside corners.

Lark's Head Knot

The Lark's Head Knot is used for a fringe edge or for attaching a hanging loop.